Oceans Apart

Oceans Apart

Stories of Overseas Evacuees in World War 2

PENNY STARNS

Dedicated to the memory of Margaret Hill-Smith

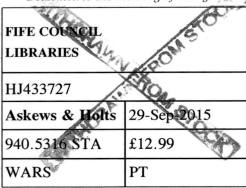
Cover images: Evacuee children. *Front cover*: Monica B. Morris Archives; Wikimedia Commons; *Back cover*: Wikimedia Commons.

First published 2014

The History Press
The Mill, Brimscombe Port
Stroud, Gloucestershire, GL5 2QG
www.thehistorypress.co.uk

British Library Cataloguing in Publication Data.
A catalogue record for this book is available from the British Library.

isbn 978 0 7524 9011 3

Typesetting and origination by The History Press
Printed in Great Britain

Contents

	Acknowledgements	6
	'There'll Always Be an England'	7
	Introduction	9
1	The Ties that Bind	13
2	The Children's Overseas Reception Board	21
3	Good British Stock	33
4	The SS *City of Benares*	46
5	American Resolve	58
6	Voyages	68
7	Communications	79
8	Maintaining National Identity	88
9	Sea-Vacs in Canada	98
10	Australian Sea-Vacs	108
11	Kiwi Brits	118
12	South Africa	126
13	Homecomings	134
14	Success or Failure	146
	Bibliography	156
	Index	157

Acknowledgements

Firstly I would like to thank my editor Sophie Bradshaw and the production team at The History Press for their excellent work. I also thank my PhD supervisor Professor Rodney Lowe for initially guiding my research into child welfare. In addition I am very grateful to all of the ex-sea-vacs who recounted their individual experiences in the form of oral history testimonies, and to the various ships' escorts, host family members and childcare professionals who documented their stories. These fascinating accounts have added a richness and depth to the overall text. I also extend special thanks to the archivist Anthony Richards of the Imperial War Museum, who assisted my research, and to the many archivists who helped me to find further information in both the national and county archives across the country, and beyond into the realms of Empire.

I thank my father Edward Starns for his love and continuing support, and my friends Timothy Dowling, Maggie Keech, Deborah Evans, Jo Denman, and Catherine Nile for their encouragement. I also appreciate my brother Christopher for his previous research assistance. Finally I thank my sons and grandchildren for their love and humour.

'There'll Always Be an England'

I give you a toast Ladies and Gentlemen
I give you a toast Ladies and Gentlemen
May this fair land we love so well
In dignity and freedom dwell

While worlds may change and go awry
Whilst there is still one voice to cry!
There'll always be an England
While there's a country lane
Wherever there's a cottage small
Beside a field of grain

There'll always be an England
While there's a busy street
Wherever there's a turning wheel
A million marching feet
Red white and blue
What does it mean to you?

Surely you're proud
Shout it out loud
Britons awake!
The Empire too
We can depend on you

Freedom remains
These are the chains
Nothing can break
There'll always be an England
And England shall be free
If England means as much to you
As England means to me

Composed and written by Albert Rostron Parker and Charles Hugh Owen
Ferry in the summer of 1939. The song became a hit for Vera Lynn during
the Second World War, and it was adopted by the sea-vacs as their signature
tune when leaving and approaching ports, and most poignantly when they
were in their lifeboats awaiting rescue after their ships had been torpedoed
by the enemy.

Introduction

Much has been written in recent years of the horrors of forced child-migration schemes; of children who were sent to the Dominions in order to work the land and boost population numbers. Often they were badly treated and exploited in the process.[1] The story of children who were sent overseas during the Second World War however, was dramatically different. This cohort of children were generally fussed over, feted, adored and completely spoilt; they were viewed as special and treated accordingly. Known as sea-vacs, the history of these extraordinary youngsters is complex and controversial. The subject matter embraces the pressing concerns of the British at war, but also highlights the prevailing social attitudes with regard to class distinctions, child welfare, eugenics, religious affiliations and national identities. In the wider sense, the topic also sheds light on the shifting sands of competing social and political ideologies within the British Empire and the strenuous efforts that were made to strengthen and uphold traditions of colonial rule. Indeed, during the months leading up to the war some sections of British society chose to make full use of colonial ties and were already abandoning the country faster than rats leaving a sinking ship.

Upper-class British families began sending their children overseas in the latter part of 1938. Some already had family connections in the United States of America or in the Dominions, and were therefore able to rely on a reasonable welcome and accommodation for their children. By virtue of their affluence, all of these families were able to secure private shipping arrangements. According to *The Times* newspaper, thousands of these wealthy children had been shipped abroad in the months leading up to the declaration of war, and during the forty-eight hours immediately before this declaration 5,000 adults and children had fled from Southampton to the

United States of America.[2] Furthermore, long queues of chauffeur-driven cars, the titled and well-to-do, accompanied by their valets and maids staggering under the weight of their luggage became a prominent feature of all British ports. Alongside these privately secured escape routes, companies such as Kodak and Ford established their own evacuation schemes. Notable academics in Canada and the USA even operated eugenically motivated evacuation programmes designed to support and preserve the intellectual elite by persuading scholars to offer homes to the children of Cambridge or Oxford dons.

Naturally, this rapid exodus of the British social, financial and intellectual elite prompted deep resentment in other sections of society. The average shipping fare from Britain to the United States was somewhere between fifteen and eighteen pounds. For around 75 per cent of the British population this amount constituted their monthly wage, and effectively priced them out of the market in terms of sending their children abroad. However, by April 1940 public criticism of elitist escape routes, combined with a significant shift in wartime circumstances, galvanised the government into action. While politicians hotly debated the pros and cons of sending children overseas, it was the imminent threat of invasion that drove policy decisions at this stage. Therefore a Children's Overseas Reception Board was established, and British children were subsequently sent to far-flung corners of the Empire.

Some sea-vacs did not arrive at their destination because their ships were torpedoed en route by the Germans, but most duly arrived on foreign shores with their meagre belongings in brown paper bags. As they lined up against the harbour walls they resembled small packages – little bundles of confused and apprehensive children. Moreover, from this point on, the experiences of sea-vacs varied enormously. For instance, one young girl found herself taking tea with Einstein, while another girl was forced to take up residence in a brothel. Some were orphaned and adopted by their host families. Others were told that they were splendid ambassadors for Britain. The majority of these children remained overseas for the duration of the war, and they attempted to maintain their sense of British identity along with their family ties. To this end, efforts were made to keep children in touch with their families through the BBC World Service. For most, however, by the time they returned to their own families they had adopted the accent and culture of their host country. This resulted in a resounding clash of personal lifestyles and expectations on their return to Britain, and a strange sense of not belonging to the mother country anymore. This book documents the rationale behind the sea-vac policy, the hopes and fears of sea-vacs, their joys and woes and their perceptions of their host countries.

Sources

The text of this book relies heavily on the primary source materials that are held at the British National Archive at Kew, London, Australian, Canadian, New Zealand and South African Government Archives, and those held at the Imperial War Museum. At the National Archive, Dominion records, especially the DO/131 series, have been particularly useful since they document the official history of the Children's Overseas Reception Board. Ministry of Health, Ministry of Education, Ministry of Home Security and Ministry of Labour records have also been consulted. The Hansard House of Commons Parliamentary Debates 5th Series has been an illuminating source of information, particularly the debates of 1939 onwards. The Imperial War Museum contains a wealth of information in the form of diaries, memoirs, private papers and the letters of children who were evacuated overseas. Collectively they have revealed an extraordinary chain of events, from the outbound voyages of young children leaving Britain to their host family experiences and their eventual homecomings at the end of the war. The Imperial War Museum also holds the Patricia Lin collection, which contains 127 overseas evacuee questionnaires. Secondary source material is listed in the select bibliography at the end of this book. The main secondary works consulted, however, are Michael Fethney's book *Absurd and the Brave* (1990), Edward Stokes' *Innocents Abroad* (1994) and Geoffrey Shakespeare's autobiography *Let Candles Be Brought In* (1949).

Notes

1   In November 2009 the Australian Prime Minister Kevin Rudd formally apologised to the adults who as children were forcibly removed from their orphanages in Britain and transplanted in Australia. Most of these forced migrations were instigated by children's charities and Dominions governments, particularly Canada and Australia.

2   *The Times*, 1 September 1939.

1

The Ties that Bind

Offers to provide an overseas refuge for British children for the duration of the Second World War were received by the British government in the spring of 1939. These offers were extended primarily by the Dominions, such as Canada and Australia, but the United States of America also offered to take children. Even Latin American countries were keen to offer help in this respect. However, most British politicians at this stage viewed overseas evacuation as unnecessary, potentially expensive and probably unwieldy in terms of administration. Furthermore, for some people the very notion of sending children overseas smacked of defeatism, and ministers argued that it was tantamount to waving a white flag before the war had even started. These early offers of help, therefore, were virtually dismissed out of hand. At this point government ministers were reasonably confident that their home front civil defence policies, which included a framework of air raid-precautions shelters and wardens, Voluntary Aid Detachment nurses and blackout procedures, would provide adequate protection from aerial bombardment. The cornerstone of civil defence measures however, relied on the systematic movement of city children and other vulnerable civilians to areas of relative safety in the countryside. This planned mass evacuation was referred to officially as the government's dispersal policy, and ministers were in the process of persuading the general public that domestic civilian evacuation was the best possible course of action should war break out.

Nevertheless, the issue of overseas evacuation was discussed at length in the House of Commons, and it is clear from early debates on the subject that politicians had a number of concerns and prejudices with regard to sending children abroad. Some of these were sensible and pertinent, while others were highly amusing. For instance, there was a general consensus within the corridors of power that British children should not be sent to Latin American countries because English was not the first language. Yet this consideration did not appear to have influenced domestic internal evacuation, whereby hundreds of Liverpool children were sent to Welsh-speaking North Wales. However, the decision to refuse offers of help from Latin American countries was viewed as a sensible one, not simply because of language difficulties but also because these countries did not have strong political or economic ties with Britain. Prevailing political opinion regarded governments in these countries as unstable and potentially volatile. A large number of politicians were also wary about sending children to Australia. During the nineteenth century, Australia had been first and foremost a penal colony. British prisons during this period were overcrowded and overflowing, and thousands of criminals were condemned to penal servitude in Australia as an alternative to incarceration in Britain. Given this association, a few officials vehemently argued that sending children to live in Australia with a bunch of convict descendants was not an appropriate course of action.

In stark contrast, Canada and South Africa were considered to be ideal destinations for good British stock should the need for overseas evacuation arise. The populations of these countries were regarded as decent, hard-working and of thoroughly good stock. Strangely perhaps, in view of Britain's long standing special relationship with the USA, politicians in Whitehall shied away from the idea of sending children to America. Their reluctance appeared to be based on the prevailing view that American children were spoilt, rude, arrogant, ill-disciplined and loud. Members of parliament also expressed a dim view of the average American mother. According to the parliamentary records of 1939 and 1940, American mothers were described as lazy, materialistic and vain. Amusing stereotypes labelled them as gossipy women who were ignorant, superficial and totally lacking in child-rearing skills. They were further considered to be loud, aggressive, ignorant, overindulgent, and petulant, whereas the demure middle- and upper-class English rose mothers were praised for being quiet and reserved in their thinking and diligent in their mothering. Even English working-class mothers were venerated when compared to their counterparts in the United States. Rear Admiral Beamish, for example, was very critical of the American lifestyle, and most vociferous on this point. During a debate of the Dominions Office Supply Committee he strongly ridiculed American mothers, claiming, 'There is a very good apple grown in this country known as the American mother. The reason it is called an American mother is that it only has one pip.'[1]

The rear admiral then went on to express that, in his view, American children were usually in charge of their mothers rather than the other way around. His view prompted murmurs of agreement and a good deal of support, but it was not shared by all. Indeed, during the same debate Major Braithwaite poured scorn on such stereotypical attitudes and declared them to be most unhelpful. He stated:

> I do not think that this is the sort of thing that ought to be said to the Committee at this time. America has shown herself our friend and is willing to give us all the armaments she can, and to cast any aspersion in that direction is something I bitterly resent.[2]

Nevertheless, these stereotypes, however unfair or inaccurate they proved to be, did serve to block any official government moves to send British children directly to the USA during the war. In fact the majority of British government officials decided that should it become necessary to send children overseas then the Dominions would be the preferred destination, since this measure would serve to strengthen pre-existing ties between Britain and her Empire.

The initial reluctance to send children overseas by means of any organised and officially endorsed scheme did not deter well-to-do families from sending their offspring overseas by private means. Between 20,000 and 30,000 children were evacuated overseas for the duration of the war. Many of them left Britain before the war broke out and did so in sporadic droves. An estimated 5,000 people left Britain's shores over the two-day period immediately prior to the declaration of war on 3 September 1939. This upper-class exodus included a large number of parents, nannies and grandparents. The Thames Valley in the September of 1939 was filled with men and women of all ages, in various stages of hunger, exhaustion and fear, offering absurd sums for accommodation in already overcrowded houses and even for food. This horde of satin-clad pinstriped refugees poured through for two or three days, eating everything that was for sale, downing all the spirits in the pubs, and then vanished.[3]

Large companies such as Warner Brothers, Kodak, Ford and Hoover also provided a means of escape by paying for the overseas evacuation of children belonging to their British employees. American universities did their part too, offering refuge to the children of leading academics working within British universities. Not surprisingly this elitist escapism became an emotive issue, and the brutal unfairness of the situation was hammered home by the increasing number of newspaper articles that focused on the wonderful lives that children were enjoying on the other side of the Atlantic.

J.B. Priestley, the famous writer and broadcaster, recalled his thoughts on the subject on his first day of duty with the Home Guard:

I remember wishing that we could send all our children out of this island, every boy and girl of them, across the sea to the wide Dominions, and turn Britain into the greatest fortress the world has known; so that then, with an easy mind, we could fight and fight these Nazis until we broke their black hearts.[4]

Another contemporary observer described the problem succinctly:

Why should the son of a rich man sleep in security in New York's gay lighted towers, the roar of traffic bound on peaceful errands in his ears, while the son of the poor man dozed in crowded shelters below our dangerous cities, menaced by the bomber's drone? It was unfair; and something needed to be done about it.[5]

Although the inequitable nature of private overseas evacuation schemes was obvious to all, public opinion was divided over the issue of sea-vacs. The fact that adults were fleeing Britain was particularly frowned upon. Undoubtedly a few sections of the population were resentful and felt deprived because they were not afforded the same opportunity to leave the country, but the majority viewed adult sea-vacs as lily-livered cowards. According to the national press, they were abandoning Britain in her hour of need, and if they were prepared to run away from danger then the country was well rid of such despicable people, while politicians maintained that since all adults were desperately needed for the war effort, any large-scale departure from Britain's shores should be avoided.

Whilst the population as a whole took a dim view of adult emigration at this time, opinion was more cohesive with regard to the subject of child sea-vacs. Over 80 per cent of the population suggested that it was appropriate for the British government to send children overseas out of harm's way. This overwhelming support for a government overseas evacuation programme was rather surprising, since domestic evacuation turned out to be a dismal failure. Less than 50 per cent of parents took advantage of the government's dispersal policy, which was implemented on the last day of August and the first two days of September in 1939, and 90 per cent of these evacuees were back in the cities by Christmas the same year.[6] Therefore, it seemed rather incongruous that parents were prepared to send their children to the far-flung corners of the Empire while simultaneously refusing to send their children to areas of relative safety in rural Britain. Government ministers, who were naturally disappointed with the failure of their dispersal policy, resolved to go back to the drawing board and initiate further domestic evacuation schemes on an ad hoc basis in the coming months.

By the spring of 1940, however, the war had taken an unexpected turn. On 12 May Germany invaded France, and Britain's main ally succumbed rapidly to enemy attack. Winston Churchill took over from Neville Chamberlain as Prime Minister, and on 26 May the Dunkirk retreat began. Subsequently, nearly 900 ships, many of them privately owned, brought 338,226 troops safely back to Britain. The combination of the fall of France and the dire plight of the British Expeditionary Force in Dunkirk prompted fears of an imminent invasion. Suddenly, overseas evacuation seemed not only an attractive proposition but a wholly desirable one in terms of saving the British race. Thus when the Dominions and the United States of America renewed their offers of hospitality, overseas evacuation became, for the first time, a serious option.

The Under Secretary of State for Dominion Affairs Geoffrey Shakespeare was given the task of constructing an inter-departmental committee to 'consider offers made from overseas to house and care for children, whether accompanied or unaccompanied, from the European war zone, residing in Great Britain, including those orphaned by war, and to make recommendations thereon'.[7]

Members of Parliament duly resurrected the debates of 1939 and raised new arguments for Geoffrey Shakespeare to consider. Indeed, from the outset he was forced to tread a careful path. Recalling his dilemma he noted:

> I was warned through a high Treasury authority that the policy was unpopular and that I should be well advised to tread delicately. Here was a dilemma. If we failed to evacuate children at a rate that the public thought necessary we should be charged with muddle and inefficiency. If we succeeded in accelerating the pace, those in high places would become restive and perhaps put an end to evacuation altogether. Those of us who were charged with the responsibility of the scheme were therefore in a somewhat invidious position, but we were so inspired with the rightness of our task and the need for urgency that we went ahead with all speed.
>
> In justice to the War Cabinet, I can frankly state that I understood why they should take a more sober view of this experiment. In the early stages the response to the announcement that a scheme had been worked out for the evacuation of children was so instantaneous and overwhelming that it revealed a deep current of public apprehension. Questions of national morale were involved.[8]

From an analysis of House of Commons debates in 1940, the prospect of sending children overseas was wholly justified on the grounds that they were either 'useless mouths', 'potential saviours' or 'ambassadors for Britain'.

It was not surprising that, at a time of strict food rationing and substantial material shortages, transporting children overseas was seen as a sensible option, since they could not contribute in any way to the overall war effort. Military personnel also endorsed the notion, albeit with a few reservations. Army chiefs welcomed the idea on the grounds that it would lift military morale if soldiers knew that their children were safely accommodated thousands of miles away from the European conflict. They also stated categorically that if Britain was invaded, children who were left in cities could potentially get in the way of fighting, or perhaps even be taken as prisoners and used as hostages by the enemy. From a military standpoint, therefore, it seemed that an official overseas evacuation plan had received the thumbs up. Only the Admiralty voiced concerns, claiming that they were unable to guarantee safe passage for children once they embarked on their ocean voyages. Admiralty chiefs stated that they were only able to provide Royal Naval ships as escorts for part of the journey, and pointed out that all ocean-bound journeys were fraught with danger. This claim was not pure rhetoric, because at this stage in the war Britain was losing sixty-six ships a month on average.

Whilst the notion of getting rid of useless mouths dominated some official thinking, with the threat of invasion uppermost in politicians' minds racial preservation also became a key concern. Eugenicist MPs argued that sending children overseas was a way of making sure that the British race survived. They maintained that if Britain actually succumbed to a German invasion these children would be potential saviours, since on reaching adulthood they would join the Dominion armed forces and continue the battle with the enemy and reclaim Britain as their own. Other MPs, including Lady Astor, viewed child sea-vacs in the role of the nation's ambassadors, who would display exemplary behaviour overseas and tug at the heartstrings of their host countries. In this way such children would rally ongoing support for the British war effort.

Churchill, however, despised the prospect of sending children overseas. He declared that the idea smacked of 'scuttling under the threat of invasion'. Furthermore, he considered it to be defeatist and beset with grave difficulties.[9]

Evidence suggests that a number of children agreed with the Prime Minister and made their feelings clear. The 10-year-old David Wedgewood Benn, for instance, wrote a letter to Churchill, which was published in *The Times*. In the letter the young David begs to be allowed to stay in England despite the forthcoming danger, against his family's plans to send him to Canada. He forcefully claimed that he would rather remain in Britain amongst the bombs than to be shipped away and desert his country.[10] Churchill enthusiastically pronounced that he was heartily cheered by the letter and responded by writing a missive to the boy's father praising his exemplary stance and virtues of national pride, courage and determination. He then sent the young David a copy of his memoirs.

Churchill firmly believed that any mass migration of children would damage the nation's morale, but his views were in the minority. The cross-party political climate had shifted and now favoured some form of official overseas evacuation scheme. Furthermore, the Under-Secretary of State for Dominion Affairs, Geoffrey Shakespeare, had prepared a detailed report that advocated the rapid implementation of overseas evacuation for children. Interestingly, however, Shakespeare chose not to sell his report to the House of Commons on the grounds of the useless mouths argument, nor on eugenically based standpoints or ambassadorial roles. Instead he encouraged politicians to view child sea-vacs in economic terms and as a method of strengthening ties between Britain and her colonies. In many respects he argued that his proposed policy was a mere economic and political trade-off – a golden opportunity that would have borne fruit even if it were not dictated by the circumstances of war. Speaking at Whitehall, Shakespeare stated somewhat lyrically:

> There is one other justification for the scheme which is in no way associated with the war. It may perhaps be one of the blessings which will flow from the war. It is still true in our national economy that exports should balance imports. We are importing into this country the fighting men of the Dominions, and we are exporting back to the Dominions the best of our children, and for this double blessing the Mother country will be forever in the debt of the daughter Dominions. This plan for evacuating children overseas is really an invisible export, because who can tell what will be the far-reaching consequences of it and what the value of it will be? It may well be that it contains within its breast the germ of a wise emigration policy for the better distribution of the population within the territories of the British Empire. That is what so many of us have been urging for so long and have prayed for. The dream is in sight of realisation. These children will form friendships, contacts and associations in the Dominions and the silken cord which binds the Empire together will be strengthened beyond all power to sever.[11]

There was an underlying assumption in Shakespeare's speech that Britain's problems were her own to resolve. Furthermore, the emotive outlining of his policy to MPs was highly influential and appealed in particular to those politicians who were against sending children to the USA. In setting out his declaration to strengthen ties with the Dominions and provide a new colonial distribution of the British race, Shakespeare had effectively established the policy course for the British government's subsequent Children's Overseas Reception Board. CORB, as it became known, was chaired by Geoffrey Shakespeare from the outset, and aimed to increase the availability of overseas evacuation for all children regardless of their social class. As he recorded in his memoirs:

> Why should the benefits of security in war time be dispensed to a selective few? If Britain was really to be a fortress, would it not be prudent to get rid of the weaker members in the fortress – the old and the young? And if there was now an opportunity of evacuating a large number of children overseas, it was idle to pretend that our war effort would be furthered by retaining them. I had always taken a special interest in problems of migration and the redistribution of population within the Empire. It would be foolish to let this opportunity slip. The clouds were surely big with mercy and were breaking with twin blessings on our heads – the gift of complete safety for our children and the resumption of migration. The only essential condition was that the scheme should be open to all alike, and no one must get the benefit of it solely by wealth.[12]

Notes

1   Hansard Parliamentary Debates House of Commons 5th Series, 2 July 1940, col. 783.
2   *Ibid.*
3   Calder, A., *The People's War* (1971) p. 36.
4   Henderson, M., 'North American Evacuation: a good idea or a bad mistake?' in *Children: The Invisible Victims of War* (2008) p. 97.
5   *Ibid.* p. 96.
6   For a detailed analysis of the British Government's civil defence and evacuation policy see Starns, P., *Blitz Families: The Children Who Stayed Behind* (2012).
7   Report of the Inter-Departmental Committee on the Reception of Children Overseas (Cmd.6213) National Archives CAB 67/7/172, Minutes, 15 June 1940; Official CORB History DO 131/43.
8   Shakespeare, G., *Let Candles Be Brought In* (1949) p. 265.
9   National Archives CAB 65/7/174 21 June 1940 & CAB 65/8/179, 1 July 1940.
10 *The Times*, 4 July 1940. David Wedgewood Benn is the younger brother of the post-war Labour MP Tony Benn.
11 Hansard Parliamentary Debates House of Commons 5th series, 2 July 1940, col. 714.
12 Shakespeare, G., *Let Candles Be Brought In* (1949) pp. 243–4.

2

The Children's Overseas Reception Board

As a Liberal MP and chairman of the CORB, Geoffrey Shakespeare was a man of great integrity, enthusiastic in his approach to work and meticulous in his planning. Given the task of considering the offers made from overseas to take British children he pursued his remit with vigour and clarity. He appointed Mr Arthur Mullins, who was the Permanent Secretary to the Department of Overseas Trade, as Director General of the new board of CORB and Mrs Marjorie Maxse, who had hitherto been the chief organiser of the Conservative Party, was given the task of making welfare arrangements. With a clear vision of how the scheme should be implemented, Shakespeare worked assiduously on the finer details and on 17 June 1940 he presented his recommendations in this respect to the War Cabinet as follows:

- Children evacuated overseas should be between the ages of five and fifteen.
- All children should be school children.
- At least ninety per cent of children should be selected from grant-aided schools.
- Parents of grant-aided schoolchildren would be required to pay six shillings a week to host families but transport overseas would be free.
- Parents of school children in the private sector would be required to pay one pound a week to host families.
- Preference should be given to children from designated evacuation areas (children in cities most at risk from bombing).
- Ideally, the scheme should include more children from poorer families.
- Children sent overseas would be fostered by host families.

- Parents needed to understand that under the government scheme children would remain overseas until war had ceased. They would however, be given free passage back to Britain at the earliest opportunity after the war.[1]

Whilst Shakespeare was in the process of outlining his detailed recommendations, news of the French surrender reached the War Cabinet. Thus Cabinet members quickly turned their attention to this latest dramatic turn of events, and the plan to evacuate children abroad was seemingly endorsed by default. As Shakespeare noted in his memoirs:

It can readily be imagined how all interest in the evacuation of children was eclipsed by the stark magnitude of this momentous event. It was often said of Maurice Hankey (later Lord Hankey), when he was Secretary to the War Cabinet, that after a completely inconclusive discussion he managed to record in the minutes such measure of agreement as there was. Cabinet Ministers were often surprised on reading the minutes to find what decisions had been taken. The Cabinet minutes on this occasion recorded the endorsement of the Children Overseas Reception Scheme. But if I were asked for a frank opinion, I should say that Winston Churchill did not appreciate what had happened; and I, for one, would not blame him. He was present while I unfolded the plan, but only present in the sense that his body was sunk in the Prime Minister's chair. His spirit was far away – soaring over the battlefields of France and witnessing her dying agony.

At a later date, when the scheme was in full swing, Mrs Winston Churchill rang me from number ten Downing Street to ask whether I could stop the evacuation of her husband's great niece, Sally Churchill. Some comment had appeared in the press that the children or grandchildren, nephews and nieces of prominent public men were among those sent overseas. One could imagine the enormous propaganda effect, in the unscrupulous mouth of Lord Haw Haw, if it were announced to the world that a Churchill had fled to the USA, and how the story might have been embroidered by an announcement that Winston Churchill was making arrangements to follow suit! It appeared that Mrs X, in the kindness of her heart, had included in the party of her own children to be evacuated Mr Churchill's great niece. Mr Churchill knew nothing about it. Could I help? If the pass-port had been issued could I get it withdrawn? If she was on the ship could I take her off? I promised to ring back in half an hour. The telephone buzzed. I discovered the whereabouts of Sally Churchill and her pass-port was withheld.

I doubt if the Prime Minister was ever in favour of the scheme from its inception. I do not criticise him for his opinion. The virtue of his leadership was that he was always a fighter, and to him the prospect of a fight on British soil was 'one fight more – the best, and the last!' He was therefore, opposed to any policy that would give the slightest impression of the weakening of national morale, such as would have resulted from any whole scale evacuation of children overseas.[2]

Undoubtedly the minutes of the meeting suggest that approval for the scheme was assumed rather than stated. Certainly Churchill's opposition was not voiced at this meeting, though a few days later he told his fellow War Cabinet members, 'a large movement of this kind encourages a defeatist spirit, which is entirely contrary to the true facts of the position and should be sternly discouraged.'[3]

Churchill did however acknowledge that it was acceptable for a limited number of children to be sent overseas.[4] Therefore, while some scholars have maintained that Churchill would have opposed the implementation of an overseas evacuation scheme outright if he had not been so preoccupied with events unfolding in France, this was simply not the case. It is obvious that Shakespeare was given the task of planning for overseas evacuation because the Prime Minister and other government ministers intended to seriously consider this migration as a feasible option, particularly when they were faced with the imminent threat of a German invasion. Even in his famous and uplifting 'we will fight them on the beaches' speech, Churchill stated with absolute certainty that should the need arise Britain would continue to fight against the Nazis by using Dominion forces. Sending British children to the Dominions, therefore, was a means of strengthening this resolve and a way of preparing these same children for the task of fighting for their country from across the seas. In fact, an analysis of parliamentary papers reveals that the Prime Minister was reasonably content for the scheme to go ahead, but only if it was strictly regulated in terms of numbers of children. He did not want to send out a signal to the world that Britain was lessening her resolve, but he was eager to squash the idea that only the rich were able to send their offspring overseas. Speaking in the House of Commons on 18 July 1940, he maintained that:

His Majesty's Government have been deeply touched by the kindly offers of hospitality received from the Dominions and the United States. They will take pains to make sure that in the use that is made of these offers there shall be no question of rich people having an advantage, if advantage there be, over poor.[5]

Shakespeare also doggedly shared this standpoint and condemned eugenicist MPs who argued that upper-class schoolchildren should be given priority within the CORB scheme in order to preserve racial integrity. Indeed,
Shakespeare's response to such suggestions was swift and firm. He defended
his egalitarian approach by stating:

> I have seen it suggested in some quarters that it would be a good policy if
> some of our public schools, whose names are rich in tradition, tore up their
> roots here and settled down overseas. That has been urged even in respect
> of schools situated, as most of them are, in the less vulnerable areas of
> this country. The Government is fundamentally opposed to such a policy.
> Even if such a policy were desirable, which it is not, there can never be, in
> time of war, the available shipping capacity. Nothing would so undermine
> public morale as to grant such facilities to the privileged few. Such a policy
> would militate against the spirit of resolution and tenacity with which we
> intend to prosecute this war.[6]

Shakespeare did attempt to appease eugenicists by highlighting the pioneering spirit of the British people and their children, but he made it clear that he
did not share their views in any shape or form. He was adamant that CORB
should consist of a cross section of children. Furthermore, most of his recommendations received a warm welcome in the House of Commons. Aside
from a small minority who continued to argue that the selection of children
should be conducted on eugenic grounds, the only other objection was about
the age range of children. The recommendations had specified that selected
children should fall into the 5–15 age group but politicians were unanimous
in stating that 14 and 15 year olds should stay behind and help with the
war effort. Agriculture and industry were desperately short of labour and
older children were easily and quickly absorbed into these occupations. In
the event, over 80 per cent of children selected were under the age of 12.
Shakespeare was insistent that his scheme would reflect all classes of children and those selected would have the very best opportunities that the
Dominions could offer. Recording the organisation of the scheme he stated:

> We chose the name CORB because the initials gave us the good monosyllabic
> word. CORB children they were called and CORB children they remained.
> Every child who left our shores carried a boot lace around its neck with
> a magic disc bearing its CORB number, framed in a substance claimed to
> be proof against salt water, and so strongly made as to be indestructible.
> Little did the makers reckon with the curiosity and destructive genius of
> our young migrants! Nevertheless, it was the outward and visible symbol

of the great adventure, on which each child was embarked, and it was rare that the child could not repeat, without looking at the disc, its own magical number. So the children became CORB children, and it was easy in discussion to identify the beneficiaries of the scheme by this crisp title.[7]

On 20 June 1940 details of the official CORB overseas evacuation scheme were released to the national press. By 11 a.m. over 3,000 people were lined up outside the CORB central office in London waiting patiently to sign their children up for the scheme. Compared to the response to the government's domestic dispersal policy, the reaction to the CORB scheme was phenomenal, and the popularity of CORB prompted alarm in official circles. Fear of invasion combined with the prospect of potentially achieving total safety for their children in foreign lands instead of the relative safety offered by domestic evacuation plans ensured widespread support. Moreover, while hosts in British reception areas were legally bound to take in evacuees whether they wanted them or not, overseas hosts were volunteers. Undoubtedly this distinction influenced parents who were understandably more inclined to send their children to hosts that actually wanted to look after their children, rather than those who were compelled by law to take them.

However, the clamour to register children for the CORB scheme exceeded all expectations. The number of applicants had reached 211,548 by 4 July; there were 199,746 from grant-aided schools and 11,702 from independent schools. Applicants continued to pour like torrential rain into the official CORB offices and the number of administrative staff needed to answer enquiries and organise travel arrangements rose from thirty to 620. In view of the vast number of applications received, Shakespeare was asked to stress the perils that were associated with sea travel. In a statement to the press he pointed out that the government did not have enough shipping to send scores of thousands of children overseas and a mass migration was not something that the government would encourage.[8]

On the same day the whole CORB scheme was temporarily halted to ensure that numbers were limited. A press statement followed, which claimed that government offices had been snowed under with letters from parents eager to register their children as sea-vacs. In fact, the news article made it clear that CORB already had far more registrations than it could cope with. This statement effectively stopped all further applications.

Shakespeare also did his best to subdue the number of registrations by stressing the perils which the children would face once they were at sea. He was not specific, but references to the dangers of long-haul ocean travel at a time when British shipping losses were high were only thinly veiled. Shakespeare's priority was to secure safe passage for children travelling to

in ruling out posture problems and foot deformities. Cases of head and body lice, along with scabies, were treated immediately before departure. Around 300 potential sea-vacs failed to pass their medical examinations and were sent home from the ports. For those who remained, further precautions were taken in terms of vaccination programmes. There also seemed to be a medical obsession with the bowel movements of potential sea-vacs; hundreds of them were dosed with large quantities of castor oil on a daily basis, and older children were introduced to the foul-tasting liquid that was known as senna tea. CORB children hoping to travel overseas congregated at the ports of departure and were generally housed on camp beds in schools while they waited to board ships.

In the meantime Shakespeare had advertised, interviewed and trained a large number of people to act as escorts for the sea-vacs on their voyages. The Salvation Army played a substantial role in obtaining escorts, who, according to Shakespeare, needed to be:

> Good sailors, under the age of fifty-five, and have experience in working with, and controlling children. Ideal candidates for the post of child escorts were people such as Life Guards and Youth Leaders who were already used to leading young children. They also needed to be available at a moment's notice.[11]

The ratio of child escorts to sea-vacs during the voyages was one escort per fifteen children. Medical staff aboard ship consisted of one doctor and two qualified nurses for every 100 CORB children. The pastoral care framework also included religious ministers and a number of teachers. Finding suitable escorts for sea-vacs was not difficult, since the number of applicants exceeded 19,000. Finding suitable shipping, however, proved to be a huge problem.

Initially, CORB officials attempted to make use of a mercy ship initiative that was introduced by the Americans. President Roosevelt passed the Mercy Ship Bill in 1940 and American officials approached Germany to ask them for safe-passage permits. At one stage an American ship was earmarked to cross the Atlantic to fetch 2,000 British children but the voyage was thwarted by dreadful weather and suspicious British officials. Consequently the ship remained in port. The Germans had assured America that they would not bomb or block American mercy ships carrying evacuees. However, British officials were certain that Germany would not honour such assurances. Since America was not yet part of the war, they also believed that Germany would begin to demand food and equipment from America in exchange for safe-passage permits.

Germany was also suspicious of American intentions. America had already refused to send food supplies to Europe in an attempt to remain neutral. But mercy ship plans to rescue British children effectively undermined American neutrality. By saving British children while simultaneously allowing French and German children to potentially die of hunger, America had shown her true allegiance. As a result, alongside the safe-passage assurances Germany also expressed deep regret that America should see fit to abandon their neutrality and pin their flag to the British cause. Yet from a British standpoint, given the circumstances and German rhetoric, it became impossible to take full advantage of the mercy ship scheme. Relying on German safe-passage assurances was never an option.[12] Nonetheless, there were those who believed that, at the very least, British children would tug at the heartstrings of Americans and elicit more support for the British war effort. The British ambassador in Washington, Lord Lothian, certainly endorsed this latter viewpoint. He firmly believed that the plight of British children would influence public opinion in Britain's favour, and prompt gifts of armaments and other equipment to assist the country's war aims.

Amid the international hotbed of political machinations, the CORB administration steered a steady course. Since the American mercy ship option was so fraught with difficulties, Shakespeare was forced to hire Dutch shipping to evacuate CORB children. Nevertheless, disappointingly for Shakespeare, Dutch shipping lines were quick to exploit the international situation and hiked up their prices dramatically. Speaking to members of the Foreign Office, Shakespeare condemned the Dutch profiteering: 'It does not seem quite right that the Dutch, whose future existence as an independent state depends on our war effort, should try to profiteer out of British government plans for evacuation.'[13]

Later Shakespeare complained:

Ships in war time are as diffident and erratic as girls with whom we are in love. They are neither reliable nor punctual. They are due at one port and turn up at another. Ships which were booked to carry our children were often sunk or damaged and alternative plans had accordingly to be made.[14]

Whilst Shakespeare was comparing wandering ships to his love life, the Dutch held firm over the sudden rise in their prices. They argued that the extra cost was unavoidable because all sea journeys would take almost twice as long as they did in peacetime. To some extent this was a valid argument. Voyages were indeed extended by days, and sometimes weeks, as ships captains attempted to evade enemy attacks and navigate minefields. There was also a dilemma facing Shakespeare and his colleagues at CORB, as he noted at the time:

The most difficult decision to take was that concerning the provision of
security for the children when sailing on the high seas. I felt a tremendous
responsibility for those entrusted to our care and the need for making
every possible provision for their safety. We could send them in unescorted
fast liners. Very few of these had yet been sunk. Alternatively we could
choose a slower ship in an escorted convoy. It was a difficult decision
to make. If we chose the fast liners the number of available ships was
greater and the rate of evacuation would be speeded up. Nevertheless,
it was clear that if one was torpedoed casualties might be high, as there
would be no escort in sight to pick up survivors. Early in July therefore,
we sought advice from the War Cabinet on this question. About this time
the *Arandora Star* carrying thousands of internees to Canada was sunk,
with heavy loss of life, and as a result we were instructed not to dispatch
children except in convoy. To this extent the suspension of our scheme
was modified.

By arrangement with the shipping companies we prescribed a low
maximum number of children to be sent with one ship. This decision
naturally reduced the rate of evacuation. The most elaborate routine
was introduced under the rules of made by the Ministry of War and the
Ministry of Transport, so that the children, once they had embarked,
should have as much boat drill as possible, both before and after sailing.
By agreement with the Admiralty we also made careful arrangements for
the earliest information to be given by day or night in case of any accident
befalling the children's ship. By the end of July and throughout August
and September all the preliminaries had been completed and every week
large numbers assembled at the hostels of the ports of embarkation.
A steady provision of ships for the next few months would have led to
the dispatch of many thousands of children. One other difficulty of an
unusual kind must be mentioned. While we were working with this sense
of tremendous urgency we realised that the whole policy of evacuation
was being scrutinised with the gravest suspicion by certain members of
the War Cabinet.[15]

Shakespeare's claims of being scrutinised were not without foundation;
mutterings and misgivings with regard to the ambitions of CORB could be
heard within the corridors of power on a daily basis. The fate of the *Arandora
Star* had prompted renewed public and political criticism of overseas
evacuation. Doubts were openly expressed about whether or not children
should embark on such perilous journeys, but these were not enough to prevent the scheme from going ahead. Safety measures were implemented, and
children were given the most easily accessible cabins.

All ships carrying CORB children left ports in convoys, and the Admiralty had issued strict instructions with regard to safety. However, these same instructions also outlined certain limitations, which rested on the degree of risk involved to all shipping. For instance, if a ship was torpedoed or bombed from the air, ships bringing up the rear of the convoy could only act as rescue vessels if there was an escort ship present or if there was no further risk of attack. Ships carrying evacuees were usually only escorted for a distance of 300 miles from port; from there on in these ships continued their voyages unprotected.

Royal Navy ships were needed to guard Britain's coastline and commitments to evacuee ships were limited. Significantly, parents of sea-vacs were unaware of this crucial detail. Indeed, standard CORB letters to parents seemed to indicate that evacuee ships would be convoyed for the entire length of their voyage. It is reasonable to speculate, therefore, that a large number of parents would not have registered their children with CORB at all if they had been made fully aware of the facts.

It should also be noted that when CORB was originally formed, the idea was mooted that refugee children from Europe, particularly Jewish children, should be evacuated along with British children. By the end of July 1940 around 9,000 refugee families had applied to CORB for assistance. Roughly 7,000 of these were German and Austrian children. The others included a sprinkling of Polish, French, Belgian, Norwegian, Czech, and Dutch children. They were looked after by several refugee committees in Britain. The bulk of these children were of Jewish origin and their situations were desperate. They were frequently the offspring of parents who had been condemned to Nazi concentration camps. Despite their best efforts, however, CORB officials were not able to send foreign children overseas. A combination of red tape and guardianship issues thwarted attempts to organise host families for the refugees. Moreover, CORB did not manage to agree any form of evacuation scheme with America, and most European refugees had put America as their first choice of destination. In many respects the Jewish refugees were better off staying in Britain, as it later transpired that Jewish children who managed to escape to America were often maltreated and forced to change their identities to prevent anti-Semitic attacks.

Notes

1 National Archives, official history of the Children's Overseas Reception Board, DO 131/43/5.
2 Shakespeare, G., *Let Candles Be Brought In* (1949) pp. 245–6.
3 National Archives CAB/65/7/174, 21 June 1940.

 4 *Ibid.*
 5 Hansard Parliamentary Debates House of Commons 5th Series, oral answers, 18 July 1940.
 6 Hansard Parliamentary Debates House of Commons 5th Series, 2 July 1940, col. 713.
 7 Shakespeare, G., *Let Candles Be Brought In* (1949) p. 246.
 8 *The Times*, 1 July 1940.
 9 The private papers of Patricia Johnson, cited in Parsons, M. & Starns, P., *The Evacuation: The True Story* (1999) p. 131.
10 *Ibid.* p. 134.
11 The Salvation Army, *War Cry*, 6 June 1940.
12 Jackson, C., *Who Will Take Our Children ?* (1985) ch. 3–6
13 Geoffrey Shakespeare speaking to the Foreign Office, quoted in Jackson, C., *Who Will Take Our Children?* (1985) p. 83.
14 Shakespeare, G., *Let Candles Be Brought In* (1949) p. 256.
15 *Ibid.* p. 264.

3

Good British Stock

As the CORB scheme gathered momentum, Geoffrey Shakespeare adopted a personal approach to his small charges. He endeavoured to be at the ports of embarkation as the children prepared to board their respective ships, and even went as far as buying them all sprigs of white heather to wish them good luck on their journeys. As the children stood on the harbourside, a jovial Shakespeare addressed them all with a passionate speech. They were told to uphold their sense of national identity and the famous British bulldog spirit. Stressing their roles as ambassadors for Britain he gave them stern advice, as he recalled in his memoirs:

Children are seldom amenable to advice given in talks and lectures, but sometimes good advice, if it is well wrapped up and given in a pleasant vein, bears fruit. I usually told the children that they did not represent themselves when they were sent overseas, and therefore they could not behave as they liked. They were going as the children of Britain. They were, in fact, like British ambassadors and consequently must behave even better than they knew how. If they behaved badly people would say: 'What frightful children! Their parents in Britain cannot be worth fighting for.' On the other hand, if they behaved well, people would say 'what splendid children these are! We must do everything we can to help their parents win.' I said, too: 'When things go wrong, as they often will, remember you are British and grin and bear it.' With great care I chose four attributes, that I consider important for children, and I gave them in order of importance. 'Be truthful, be brave, be kind, and be grateful.' I sometimes added: 'You may be surprised that I put truthfulness first, but that is clearly the most important. We are fighting this war because Hitler never learned

to be truthful as a boy. Nobody trusts a word he says and so all relations
with Germany have become impossible. Exactly the same thing happens
when a boy or girl is untruthful. Nobody trusts them and they miss the
best things in life.'

CORB children were also told that since they were able to represent their
country abroad, a great honour had been bestowed upon them. They were
considered to be of good British stock and great care was taken to present such children as a crucial part of Britain's future. Behind the sprigs
of heather and uplifting speeches, however, not all was going to plan.
Shakespeare had fought long and hard to make sure that official overseas
evacuation was conducted in an egalitarian manner. He had condemned
British eugenicists and their calls for a highly selective evacuation of
Britain's brightest and best children, arguing that sea-vacs needed to consist
of a broad spectrum of children. Yet his plans in this respect were severely
undermined by the receiving countries. Australia, New Zealand, Canada
and South Africa laid down their own criteria for accepting children, driven
by their individual cultural, political and economic agendas. Furthermore,
these agendas discriminated against certain children on racial, religious
and health grounds. British eugenicists need not have been unduly concerned, therefore, because their views were already well established in, and
enforced by, the Dominion States. Moreover, in the event, the selection and
screening of CORB children was dictated by the receiving countries and not
by Shakespeare.

South Africa refused point-blank to accept any Jewish children, while
Australia stipulated that Jewish children should not make up more than
10 per cent of evacuees. Restrictions were also placed on the number of
Catholic children travelling to the Dominions, and a colour bar was in operation in most instances. Children with medical defects, however minor, or
behavioural problems were automatically excluded from the scheme.[2]

Official documents reveal that these severe restrictions were not questioned
or challenged by CORB officials, even though they went against the grain
of Shakespeare's aims and objectives, and his fundamental value system.
Already irked by what he perceived to be Dutch profiteering with regard to
transportation, Shakespeare appeared to be totally deflated by Dominion
immigration rules. The imposition of these rules was never debated in
Parliament, since the restrictions were not divulged. The numerous members
of the unwieldy advisory council of CORB refused to get involved in any frank
discussions about the process of evacuee selection. Nevertheless, although
the issue was not confronted head on, there were some indications that politicians were aware of the difficulties. Mr Lunn, MP for Rothwell, observed,

'In these cases of emigration to the Dominions, as we know, the children have to pass through a very close sieve.'[3]

While the whole process of selecting evacuees bound for foreign shores was, in theory, very limiting, in practice some children slipped through the net. This was particularly the case in instances whereby children had minor medical defects such as myopia or slight hearing problems. It is not certain whether doctors conducting the medical examinations allowed some children to slip through the net deliberately, or whether children possessing such minor medical abnormalities were accidentally overlooked. Available documentation suggests that the former scenario was a more likely one. Even so, around 11 per cent of the children who had passed medical examinations that had been conducted by British doctors failed those that were imposed by doctors chosen by the High Commissioners of the Dominions.

Certainly, officials in the receiving countries cast doubt on the efficacy of British medical examinations. One Canadian official remarked, 'Occasionally, examiners found a cretinous child on board one of the evacuation ships, causing both Canadian and American doctors to question medical screening procedures used in England.'[4]

Aside from the problems associated with evacuee selection, Shakespeare was also confronted by Dominion policy variations as to how evacuees would be monitored, not only on their arrival, but also during their overall stay, as they would require continued supervision to ensure their wellbeing. Government administrations in Australia, New Zealand and South Africa were eager to establish their own laws of guardianship to protect their young evacuees, whereas Canada insisted that Britain should assume and retain guardianship for the duration of the war. The fine-tuning of such policy decisions were still being discussed as the first CORB evacuees set sail aboard the *Anselm* on 21 July 1940 bound for Canada.

The *Anselm* left Liverpool docks in a convoy that was attacked by German U-boats a mere six days later. The *Anselm* managed to escape, but four other ships in the convoy perished. There were, of course, safety measures in place for all children on board. No child was berthed below the waterline, and organisers made sure that in most instances there was at least one adult for every three children. Safety drills with regard to the positioning of lifeboats and proper training in the prompt use of such boats was instilled in all passengers. In addition to these important safety drills, children were given basic information about the countries of their destinations. Such information included the geography of the country, its language, culture and political structure, and its religious affiliations. But for the sea-vacs, being British was all important, and this needed to be conveyed to their host parents. Britain was the mother country of the Dominions, and the relationship between

Britain and her empire was crucial to the war effort. Indeed by this stage it can be argued that the CORB evacuation programme was as much an exercise in international propaganda as it was an exercise in humanitarian rescue. Sea-vacs generally were placed with host parents who had been screened for their suitability to be guardians and who were visible in public life. In this way, sea-vacs were automatically given a high media profile and were thus able to highlight Britain's plight as a lone fortress island standing resolute against the enemy. In the receiving countries, government officials and various public figures usually held welcoming parties as the children arrived at their destinations. Newspaper articles and radio broadcasts reported on the plucky little children who had escaped the bombs of their native land to begin new lives of safety and calm.

Not all children arrived at their destinations, however, and this was not surprising in view of the number of ships that were lost during the summer of 1940. Between the beginning of July and the end of September 1940 nineteen ships had set sail with their precious cargoes of good British stock; just 90 per cent of the evacuees on board reached their destinations safely. The sea voyages were dangerous and time-consuming. During June, July and August of 1940, 152 ships were obliterated by German U-boats and a further fifteen ships were destroyed by the Luftwaffe. Ships often took twice as long to reach their destinations, as they detoured in order to avoid mines. The MS *Batory*, for example, left Liverpool bound for Australia on 6 August with 477 evacuees on board and fifty-one medical staff and escorts. The ship was forced to cross the equator on three occasions simply to avoid the mines. The vessel eventually arrived in Australia having travelled 20,000 miles instead of the usual 13,000 miles.

Some vessels were forced to return to Britain. The *Volendam* for instance, was carrying 321 children when it was bombarded by two torpedoes in the Atlantic on 1 August 1940. The damage was not severe, partly because the second torpedo failed to explode. Significantly, a young boy of 9 had been overlooked in the evacuation procedures and found himself to be the captain of the sinking ship the following morning. This fact, however, needed to be kept secret if the overseas evacuation scheme was to continue. Thus Geoffrey Shakespeare took great pains to ensure that the story was never revealed at the time, but later explained the scenario:

> It appeared that in the confusion and darkness following the submarine attack on the *Volendam* Robert, the missing boy had been left sleeping in his cabin. It was a difficult task for escorts, who had only been in charge of the children for a day, to marshal them with certainty in these circumstances. So Robert was left behind and alone, except for a nucleus of engineers who

had stayed with the ship in the hope of bringing her home. After midnight Robert woke up and found himself alone in his cabin. He went on deck and saw the boats had been launched and the ropes dangling loose. To be on a big ship of 15,000 tons in company of others is sometimes a frightening experience. For a small boy to be quite alone must have been a nightmare. Robert however, was Scottish, and of the same race that has provided leaders in every part of the British Empire. There was nothing for him to do except to return to his cabin and sleep, so he slept. In the morning the list had increased and the ship had almost turned over, but Robert explored the scene of the damage and salved a large part of the German torpedo. In the distance he saw approaching two British destroyers. At this stage he discovered the nucleus of engineers so felt less lonely. The destroyers came alongside. Robert was reluctant to leave the ship. He was in command of her. It was almost his ship. He had sailed ships on a pond in Glasgow, but he had never been to sea, and he most certainly had never been almost alone on a big ship like this. It was with difficulty that they persuaded him to be transferred to the destroyer. He finally arrived at Gourock, decorated with innumerable badges and buttons, and carrying half the German torpedo!

When I arrived at Glasgow I heard that Robert and his elder brother, who had also been on the *Volendam*, were in the hostel waiting for their father to fetch them. I gave instructions that they were not to be released until the father had called on me in my hotel. Presently the father arrived. Could I persuade him to keep Robert's story to himself? Its publication would damage our scheme. We discussed the glorious adventure of his son over a glass of sherry. I put all my cards on the table and explained my anxieties. The father was a grand type of Scotsman, reliable, trustworthy and understanding. He gave his word that the story should never be revealed. I seized his hand in a flood of gratitude.[5]

Although Shakespeare had managed to hide Robert's story, and the *Volendam* was towed back to British shores, other disasters were in the offing. It is perhaps worth noting that the *Batory* was carrying 1,000 troops in addition to evacuees, and the *Volendam* was carrying wheat as a primary export to the United States of America. Consequently, some scholars have maintained that both of these ships were legitimate targets for enemy action. However, there is no evidence to suggest that ships carrying purely evacuees would have been any less of a target than those that were carrying a wide variety of cargoes. Furthermore, at this stage, despite the obvious dangers involved in oceanic travel, even parents of children who had returned to British shores because they had experienced enemy action were still prepared to send their offspring out to sea once more. As *The Times* reported on 4 September 1940:

Mr Geoffrey Shakespeare, His Majesty's Under Secretary of State for the Dominions, 'Uncle Geoffrey' to thousands of overseas evacuees, was at a Scottish port today to see off over two hundred evacuee children from English and Welsh schools who were on board the liner torpedoed off Ireland last week. They were going to their homes and 'Uncle Geoffrey' bought up all the white heather he could obtain to present each child with a sprig, together with a written message 'Warmest congratulations and good luck, we are all proud of your bravery'.

He walked up and down the train talking to the singing and cheering children, who carried books and toys given them by their Scottish hosts, and just before the train left he bought hundreds of comics and pounds of sweets for distribution during the journey.

Luggage and other property taken from the liner will be dispatched with money belonging to the children to their parents. Most of the children loudly proclaimed their desire to have 'another go for Canada' and many parents have echoed this view.[6]

Further newspaper articles described the sea-vacs as stoical, cheerful, courageous and patriotic. In this respect, CORB children were viewed in a completely different way to domestic evacuees. Whereas the latter were part of an internal dispersal policy and scrutinised in terms of their social class, the former were viewed in terms of their national identity. Internal evacuation became a problematic domestic programme that highlighted the lower-class identities of evacuees, and the subsequent clash of social orders. Overseas evacuation was a programme of international and diplomatic significance in which the British citizenship of participants was emphasised rather than class origins. Thus, to Dominion officials, CORB children were '[not] just evacuees, transferred from the range of menace, but part of Britain's mortality, part of the greatness of her past, and part of all the hope of her future'.[7]

Perceived in this way, the children concerned did their best to live up to expectations, but the welcoming parties of dignitaries and the persistent attentions of the international press were often overwhelming. Barbara Browne, who was evacuated to South Africa, recalled her experiences of the journey and the reception:

It was one big adventure and freedom from everything. To go to a place like South Africa where the stamps had an orange tree full of oranges on them, and the wide open spaces, what more could I want? There was great excitement, especially when we saw Table Mountain. But when we arrived, in that hot sun we stood for hours listening to people welcome us and saying that we were special, that they would give us everything they could and that they were so happy that we had arrived safely. It went on and on and there we were in our Sunday best waiting to go ashore.[8]

Madge Wear, who was a CORB escort, remembered with clarity the secrecy that surrounded her departure:

I was told that I was due to go to South Africa and I must not mention it to anybody, not even my family. I was given twenty-four hours' notice of when we sailed. My poorest one [sea-vac] was called Peter Capslove and I loved him from the word go. He was a Holy terror, a real little cockney and he came with all his belongings in paper bags. I used to try and teach the children bits about South Africa and we had a few lessons on board. One Sunday we were sitting on deck and a whale appeared, spouting. As you can imagine, everybody rushed to the side of the ship.[9]

Miss Wear's testimony highlights the fact that under the CORB scheme poor children were sent overseas at the same time as their richer counterparts. Furthermore, it was not unusual for CORB children to travel alongside those who were being evacuated overseas under private schemes or family arrangements. It is clear, however, that, amid the excitement and sense of adventure, British children arriving at their various destinations were made to feel special. A series of articles published in the *British Eugenics Review* also underpinned the wider importance of these children above all others. Such articles claimed that since the Dominions were in receipt of 'good British stock' they needed to nurture these children carefully, not least because the continuation of the British race may ultimately rest on their shoulders. Not surprisingly given this sinister long-term agenda, eugenic debates consistently undermined notions of egalitarianism, and eugenicists vigorously agitated for overseas evacuation to be restricted according to fundamental eugenic principles. Frustrated by the failure of CORB to take on board these principles, members of the British Eugenics Society took matters into their own hands. They introduced their own evacuation schemes, which were based on the premise that some children were worth more than others because they were eugenically important. The British Eugenics Review stated that in order for children to be classed as 'eugenically important' they were required to meet strict criteria. Basic eugenic safeguards insisted that such children should be intelligent, healthy and of good heredity. Keen to throw off the notion that eugenically important children would, by necessity, have to be rich, the Eugenic Society of Great Britain aligned its aims with the Canadian Eugenics Society and provided a fund of money from which parents could borrow the fare of the overseas passage and pay it back at a later date.

Yet the existence of this fund was merely a theoretical way of paying lip service to the possible inclusion of children from poorer backgrounds. In practice, even a superficial assessment of the criteria for eugenically important children suggests that Madge Wear's cockney 'Holy terror' would not have been selected as one of this elite group.

As eugenicists pursued the quest for good British stock, a committee of doctors who had been approved by the Homes in Canadian Service Committee was given the job of applying fundamental eugenic principles to the selection process. It was expressly stated that the co-operation of British and Canadian Eugenic Societies would ensure that 'Provision will be made for certain eugenically important groups which do not come within the scope of the Government's evacuation scheme now being administered by the Children's Overseas Reception Board'.[10]

In the event only eighty-four 'eugenically important' children were evacuated to Canada as a result of the combined efforts of the Eugenics societies. Problems associated with shipping, exit visas and medical screening combined to thwart their attempts to formulate a large-scale evacuation. More significantly, the members of such societies began to attract negative attention. Their motives were scrutinised and their activities criticised. Officials in government and published articles in the national press began to draw distinct parallels between Hitler's policy of social Darwinism and policies advocated by eugenicists. It was deemed unseemly to refer to children as 'good British stock' as though they were breeds of cattle to be exported at will. Such references prompted an increasing sense of unease within the corridors of power and a growing recognition that eugenically based policies were at odds with British democracy. Yet it was the Canadian government that first took action against eugenicists by tightening up legislation and blocking their policies. The President of the Canadian Eugenics Society, Dr Hutton, was eventually forced to admit defeat and announced, 'The government restrictions in Canada are so severe that the Eugenics Society of Canada can no longer carry on the work and is obliged to retire from the field.'[11]

A further statement in the British Eugenics journal apologised for the demise of the Canadian eugenic movement: 'We very much regret to learn that owing to circumstances entirely beyond their control, the Eugenics Society of Canada no longer exists.'[12]

The sudden downfall of eugenically based organisations effectively ended overt eugenically motivated migrations from British shores to Canada. Henceforth, sea-vacs set sail with the help of government-sponsored, private and company schemes, and those that were implemented by receiving countries. The most successful of the latter groups was the American 'Committee for the Evacuation of European Children', which was highly efficient and resourceful. According to the records kept by Shakespeare, no children were sent to the United States under the CORB scheme. However, 838 children were sent under the auspices of the American Committee for the Evacuation of European Children, with the collaboration of CORB.[13]

The work of the Americans was significant because they were able to exert considerable influence across Europe. The USA was neutral until the bombing of Pearl Harbor by the Japanese on 7 December 1941, and their welfare officials, bound by the desire to rescue as many children as possible, organised large-scale evacuations from areas of conflict to the safety of American shores. Companies such as Kodak and Ford also initiated migrations. Indeed, to a large extent these American-led schemes eventually served to replace the efforts that had been made by CORB.

Furthermore, the Dominions, and Canada in particular, continued to receive waves of evacuees throughout the war, despite the shadow of eugenics. These influxes of children were largely due to the efforts of well-to-do middle-class Canadian women and their eagerness to help with the British war effort. Their ideas were discussed at a number of lavish garden parties, initially in Vancouver, and spread across the nation. As a result, the formation of the Canadian National Registration of Women for War Work generated offers of help from 100,000 women. Their efforts were also, in part, racially motivated, and endorsed by the National Council of Women. One prominent member, Mrs Emma J. Walker, stated categorically that, sheltered from the perils of invasion, British sea-vacs would form the nucleus of a 'New Britain' founded on British stock.[14]

Even with the demise of eugenic societies, therefore, the notion of building a 'New Britain', if necessary, from the good British stock that arrived on the shores of Dominion states on a daily basis, still carried considerable weight and public support. Despite eugenic overtones, the national press in Britain and the countries that received sea-vacs were singing from the same hymn sheet in this respect. Good British stock, living in foreign lands, had the potential to liberate Britain from her enemies. Oral history testimonies from the sea-vacs concerned, however, suggest that although some were acutely aware of their ambassadorial role, they had not considered the prospect of eventually having to fight to reclaim Britain from German invaders. In fact, nothing was further from their minds. They were simply too busy adjusting to their new surroundings to contemplate any long-term plans, and the majority were unaware that they were part of a much wider political agenda. In fact, not only were sea-vacs unaware of some of the heavy expectations that had been placed upon their small shoulders, there were suspicions that some evacuees, particularly those who were travelling by private arrangement, were actually leaving Britain to avoid having to fight at all. A fireman aboard a ship to Canada was incensed by what he saw as a movement of mass cowardice:

> Well, there were kids and a lot of Army dodgers among them ... I seen the so-called kids. Short trousers on of a day and long trousers of a night on deck. They were all the rich men's sons. Lords, Dukes, bank manager's children. I came up and out of the engine room and my face and hands were black with the dirty job I'd done. There were three of your so-called children who seen me and said 'Arn't you dirty.' I said 'F off' and go back and fight for your country.' They run ... My sisters lost a lad each in the forces, they didn't run away.[15]

Resentment against private sea-vacs was rife throughout the war, and class barriers were reinforced by the conflict. In eugenic terms, British sea-vacs drawn from the upper classes and intelligentsia were those who were considered to be good British stock. Perceived in a broad context, however, these were not necessarily the children who would consider fighting for their homeland – rather, for many, it was the exact opposite.

It can be argued, therefore, that the notion of sending good British stock abroad was used to some extent to justify the mass exodus of upper-class children. As a diplomat working in Canada House observed:

> Canada House is being invaded by women of the aristocracy wanting to send their children overseas ... they are all looking to Canada now. We are to provide them with men and ammunition, take their children, and intern their fifth column etc. Here we have a whole social system on the run, wave after wave of refugees and these are only people at the top, people who can buy titles, letters of introduction, or the ruling manner to force their way into government offices and oblige one to give them an interview. What of the massed misery that cannot escape?[16]

Certainly the need to quell working-class anger and establish some semblance of equity amidst the fleeing aristocrats had been the main impetus behind CORB. As far as Shakespeare was concerned, all British children were good British stock. He noted:

> I did my best to expound the scheme in its proper perspective in a broadcast ... but I refused, on behalf of the government, to make a decision for the parents. I asked them to decide for themselves and to weigh the dangers of the voyage against the ultimate benefits and complete security ensured. As the European horizon darkened, and the Gestapo terrorised the civil

population in all the countries conquered by the Germans, British parents preferred the short perils of the ocean to the prospect of the long drawn out terrors that confronted this country. When, however, I asked my own children, William and Judith, if they wished to go overseas, they burst into tears and emphatically refused to go. Looking back on those days I sometimes reproach myself for trying to go so fast, for in the early stages, at any rate, an almost intolerable strain was imposed upon my staff. But with the threat of impending invasion, parents naturally insisted on evacuation at the utmost speed and we were forced to abandon procedure appropriate for migration in peace. The fact that the first children's ship sailed within a month of the initiation of the scheme was proof of the zeal and dispatch with which the organisation worked.[17]

Though they had signed a disclaimer that absolved the government from any responsibility, parents of CORB children were not allowed to be present at the point of their child's embarkation. This rule was introduced to prevent unwanted displays of emotion. Although according to Shakespeare, the sight of small children setting out on their voyages was a scene that could reduce anyone to tears:

We were very wise in making it a rule that parents should not accompany their children to the port. There would have been unendurable scenes of emotion if we had allowed them to do so. The farewell scenes were heartrending enough for those who had never seen the children before. They nearly always sang, in the final stages 'There'll always be an England'. It has a patriotic lilt and is a catchy tune. But when it is sung by small children leaning over the rail of a great ship it has a profoundly moving effect. I could hardly ever hear them singing without a lump in my throat. Mr Graham Cunningham, who joined the Board, came as a hard headed businessman, with little respect for politicians, and less for civil servants. He gripped CORB, pruned off its excrescences, and made the wheels of the machinery revolve with the maximum of efficiency. I thought he was devoid of feelings until on one occasion we stood together on a small barge to wave final farewells to a crowd of CORB children, singing as usual, 'There'll always be an England!' I turned to pass a remark to Graham Cunningham, and, to my surprise, the tears were coursing down his cheeks. The poignant parting with the children revealed his real nature and that warmth of heart which he had tried so hard to conceal.[18]

Even though one-fifth of CORB children were Scottish and another fifth were Welsh, the rousing patriotic song 'There'll Always Be an England' became the signature tune of all children who were leaving British shores. It was written in 1939 and recorded by the forces' sweetheart Vera Lynn. The song captured the mood of the nation as it stood firm against German aggressors. Moreover, children sang this tune as they left British ports and again as they sailed into their destination ports. Indeed, ships laden with evacuee children became known as the 'singing ships,' and whenever they were feeling down or homesick, children and their escorts would burst into song in order to lift their spirits. They also sang when they were in trouble, as Shakespeare recounted of the survivors of the torpedoed *Volendam*:

> It appeared that the *Volendam* was torpedoed at ten o' clock at night. There was a fair wind and a heavy sea running. The children had been well practised in boat drill; and when they were ordered to assemble at their boat stations, each party of fifteen, led by its escort, proceeded as a matter of routine, even in the darkness, to the point of assembly. The lights in the ship had failed, but, despite the darkness, drill was carried out. To the children it was just another practice. They took their places in the boats and were lowered without incident, but, sad to relate, the purser fell into the sea and was drowned. One of the escorts told me that it was the most moving experience in her life, to hear in the darkness, borne on the wind, the voices of children singing, 'There'll always be an England', and 'Roll out the Barrel'. It has sometimes been urged by the opponents of the scheme that only children of low morale sought refuge overseas. This was of course a cruel slander. In the first place it was the parents who decided to send them; but the cheerfulness and courage of the children and their conduct that night in small boats, tossed about in an angry sea, were worthy of the finest traditions of our race.[19]

It seems that other people in high places were also touched by the plight of such plucky children. There were gifts of clothes, toys, sweets and other luxuries showered on the children as they set sail. Mr Simon Marks (later Sir) gave the children new clothing to the value of £7,000, and there was a magnificent gift of £25,000 from the government of Fiji.[20] As the 'good British stock' embarked on their adventures, their journeys and experiences became the focus of media attention. But as Shakespeare clearly stated, from the point of their departure the British government could no longer accept any responsibility for their fates. Moreover, as ocean-going conditions continued to deteriorate, the fortunes of such children became more uncertain.

Notes

1 Shakespeare, G., *Let Candles Be Brought In* (1949) p. 257.
2 National Archive PRO, DO131/3: *Minutes of the Children's Overseas Reception Board Advisory Council (CORB)*, 16 July 1940. See also *Official CORB history:* National Archive PRO/DO131/43: *Orders to Medical Examiners* PRO/DO35/713/M52–65.
3 Hansard Parliamentary Debates House of Commons 5th Series, 2 July 1940, col. 754.
4 Jackson, C., *Who Will Take Our Children?* (1985) p. 27.
5 Shakespeare, G., *Let Candles Be Brought In* (1949) p. 270–1.
6 *The Times*, 4 September 1940, also reported in the *Dorset Daily Echo* on the same day. Extract quoted in Parsons. M. & Starns, P., *The Evacuation: The True Story* (1999) p. 139.
7 Lin, P. 'National Identity and Social Mobility: Class, Empire and the British Government: Overseas Evacuation of Children during the Second World War', *Twentieth Century British History* Vol. 7, No. 3 (1996) p. 312. See also National Archive PRO/DO/131/45.
8 Browne, B., oral history interview conducted by the BBC (1999) quoted in Parsons, M. & Starns, P., *The Evacuation – The True Story* (1999) pp. 164–6.
9 Wear, Madge, oral history interview conducted by the BBC (1999) *Ibid.* pp. 164–5
10 *British Eugenics Review* vol. 32 April 1940–January 1941.
11 *British Eugenics Review* vol. 33 April 1941–January 1942.
12 *Ibid.*
13 Hansard Parliamentary Debates House of Commons 5th Series. Mr Geoffrey Shakespeare giving oral answers with regard to the activities of CORB, 25 February 1941, col. 374.
14 Walker, E.J., quoted in Bilson, G., *Guest Children: The Story of the British Child Evacuees sent to Canada during World War II* (1988) p. 2.
15 *Ibid.* p. 113.
16 *Ibid* p. 9.
17 Shakespeare, G., *Let Candles Be Brought In* (1949) pp. 253–5.
18 *Ibid.* p. 259–60.
19 *Ibid.* pp. 268–9.
20 *Ibid.* p. 256.

4

The SS *City of Benares*

ollowing on from the *Volendam* disaster, another catastrophe occurred in the Atlantic. Unlike the *Volendam*, however, on this occasion events were so calamitous that they could not be hushed up or played down for the sake of the overall CORB scheme. Indeed, it was a tragedy unlike any other. On 17 September 1940 at 10.30 p.m. a ship carrying CORB children and private evacuees named SS *City of Benares* was torpedoed by German U-boat U48, 600 miles from its point of embarkation in Liverpool. As a result of this attack 256 of the 406 passengers and crew aboard the *City of Benares* were killed. A total of seventy-seven CORB children who were on their way to Canada were among the dead. Six of their escorts had also died. Most of the *City of Benares* victims died before they could even move, while others perished of exposure in the bitterly cold ocean, battered by storm-force winds. Understandably this terrible incident shocked the nation and undoubtedly the event was perceived as a war crime, as the national press reported:

> The doctrine of devils finds its fiendish devotees in Adolf Hitler and his crew. There is a pang in the heart of the nation. Deep sorrow, there is, and profound sympathy with the parents of the massacred children as well as, for the moment, the hot rage and sickening indignation which is evoked by the latest atrocities of the gangsters. But not for long. The hot rage will be chilled into a colder sterner determination to put an end to this reign of terror – or to perish.
>
> It would appear that relief was only twenty four hours away from the moment of disaster. It would be wise to remember in any tightening up of the Escorts Scheme that there is now no depth of cruel savagery which the Nazi will not plumb: that there is no limit to his disregard of the rules

of civilized warfare, and that the future precautions must have full regard to those facts. In this terrible incident the quality of our children has been proved to be that of refined gold. Brave discipline, unselfish consideration of others, and unquestioning trust in their teachers and other protectors, have shone as a bright radiance in the darkness of a German savagery.[1]

On leaving Liverpool the *City of Benares* had formed part of a convoy numbered OB213 and she had been delayed for forty-eight hours because of mines in the Mersey. But for this delay the *City of Benares* may well have reached her destination unscathed. However, one of the convoy ships, the destroyer HMS *Winchelsea* was required to provide escort to another convoy HX17 travelling from Nova Scotia, which was laden with armaments for the war effort. When the *City of Benares* was attacked, therefore, she was unprotected. Furthermore, rescue vessels were nowhere to be seen. Escort policy was such that ships carrying evacuees were only escorted for a distance of 300 miles out of port. At a distance of 600 miles, the *City of Benares* had no chance of defending her position. Parents of sea-vacs had assumed that when travelling in convoy, surviving ships would automatically come to the aid of ships that were sinking, yet this was not the case. The Admiralty had issued strict instructions, which rested entirely on the degree of risk involved. Ships bringing up the rear of the convoy could only act as rescue vessels if there was an escort ship present or if there was no further risk of attack. When the *City of Benares* was attacked, therefore, other ships in what remained of the convoy abandoned the area as quickly as possible. As one survivor recalled, 'certainly in the night one didn't notice the other ships disappearing but they were right to do so'.[2]

Bess Cummings who was aboard the *City of Benares* described the moment of attack and her subsequent rescue:

There was a huge explosion at about 10.30 p.m. The entire ship shuddered, furniture fell about and wardrobes tumbled across doors, which made getting out of cabins extremely difficult. We all knew where the lifeboat stations were and we all made attempts to get there, but not all of us succeeded. Some of the children were killed before they could even move, which was very sad.

The water in my lifeboat came up to my chest, so you can imagine younger children, smaller children, had no chance. The adults who had put themselves onto the side of the lifeboat like we had began to realise that for them there was no hope of survival. It might be better just to let go and slip away and they did. On board the whaler from the *Hurricane* I could see men jumping up and down, waving at us, calling us and shouting 'Hang on girls.' To find two girls alive, on an upturned lifeboat was just amazing for them, they were crying as well as laughing.[3]

Another survivor, Lord Quinton, recalled the chaotic scenes as people fought for places on lifeboats:

We were sitting in the lounge at about ten at night, thereabouts, and I was reading an historical novel about Napoleon. There was a terrific banging noise, which sounded, where we were, more like a collision than an explosion, but it was in fact the explosion of a torpedo somewhere near the stern of the ship. Then the bells went and so on and so forth and we nipped down to our cabin and got our life jackets and put them on together with a heavy overcoat and went back to our boat station. Then absolutely nothing happened. Then a rather energetic man said 'I think we had better go to the boat.' So we all got up. Nobody came to call us. We headed off to where we knew our boat was going to be and indeed our boat was just waiting there for us, but it was a little on the full side. There were an enormous number of people in it. The crew began to lower it and then either a rope broke or somebody ran away from the winding thing, and it went. One end of it was held on by rope, the other end fell away and people fell down, and a lot of people fell out and I fell out because there was an enormous weight of people falling on top of me, so I zoomed down quite a way. I must have hit my head in the course of it on some piece of tackle hanging off the side of the ship because I was not properly conscious for a while until I bobbed up.

I fell into the sea. I came to, I suppose because of the effect of the sea, and looked around. All the lights were on in the ship and it was a scene of vigorous activity and I really thought I was done for, you know, I thought 'oh dear, well this is it!' Then, because I had forgotten I was wearing a really wholly reliable life jacket, I bounced up and stayed up and then my mother saw me from thirty yards distance I suppose, and yelled in an imperious way and I swam over to her and clambered in the boat. The boat was thoroughly water logged but it was still buoyant because of the required buoyancy tanks and when we actually drifted away at that stage of the proceedings there were twenty three people on the boat and I imagine there had been about sixty five when we hit the water, but when the boat went, when it fell, bow into the water, no stern into the water, and was completely water logged so that only the bow and stern were sticking out so that all of us in the middle were submerged. Well when the stern of the lifeboat hit the water it was completely submerged for a bit and we finished up with twenty three people when there must have been sixty or more in it and of these twenty three, I think eight were Lascar crew and fifteen were Europeans. There were five children.

People just died of exposure because it was very cold. It wasn't very nice having these bodies more or less floating around in this stuff so we, the more vigorous of the Lascars and I, eased them over the side, but we didn't do that with people who still had living relations in the boat.

There were pretty heavy seas, but they weren't too bad. You'd get a bit of warm water around you and then you would go upon one of these great waves and it would break at the top and the little bit of water you had warmed round yourself was then replaced with extremely chilly water, but I was a plump healthy youth and I certainly wasn't hideously cold, I wasn't chattering or shuddering with cold at any time. I was just cold.

I can remember moaning, 'oh God, what's going to happen next' ... Some very interesting things occurred in a way. I will never forget seeing potted plants, potted little palms that had been in the dining room, floating past in their stands, it was quite an eerie spectacle, and some people afterwards said that the submarine surfaced. It had torpedoed another ship as well and had a look round, but they didn't do anything horrible, like machine gunning the survivors. They just closed the lid and disappeared and went off for another quarry.[4]

Faced with the dreadful and tragic events that accompanied the sinking of the *City of Benares*, there were many who displayed stoical determination and heroism. Lord Quinton's mother, for example, was not prone to pessimism, even though the survivors in her lifeboat were giving up hope.

At about two o'clock the next day somebody said, 'Look a ship' and we all craned our eyes and of course at that time we had seen a number of phantom ships coming to our rescue already and had developed a certain scepticism about this. But it got longer and larger and larger and then a boat from the ship passed within hailing distance and a sailor shouted 'We will be back for you later, we are picking up people from rafts,' and then they disappeared and well, that was I say between two and three o'clock. I suppose about five o'clock we were picked up. But, in the interval a rather depressed Hungarian publisher, right in the middle of the boat nearly to his neck in water, said 'They have forgotten us, they will not come' and my mother decided to address him in pigeon English to make the message absolutely clear and said 'No, no, big ship come.'[5]

The most famous heroine associated with the *City of Benares* tragedy how-ever, was the resourceful and magnificently resilient Miss Mary Cornish.

Along with forty adults and six children, the 21-year-old CORB escort lifted the spirits of the survivors in her open lifeboat by singing well-known hymns and inventing stories to keep the children attentive and optimistic. As they took refuge under some canvas in the bows of their small vessel, Miss Cornish continually massaged the children's hands and feet to relieve them from the bitter cold. Each morning and evening she told the children gripping adventure tales, which were loosely based on the character of Bulldog Drummond.[6]

The intrepid Miss Cornish and her band of survivors were at sea in the open lifeboat for a period of eight days, 600 miles from the nearest land mass. By this stage their rations had completely gone and they were getting increasingly dehydrated and weak, battered by the gruelling Atlantic winds and the cold temperature of the ocean that surrounded them. Eventually they were spotted by a Sunderland flying ship, and another flying ship guided a British warship to the place where the hopeful survivors sat, huddled together, still singing songs to uplift their spirits. The majority of survivors were rescued by whaling ships and the Royal Navy ships HMS *Hurricane* and HMS *Anthony*. As the survivors were plucked from their lifeboats and onto the ship, they were wrapped in warm blankets and given water to drink. The dedicated crew of the rescue ship claimed that once all the survivors were safely aboard, a party atmosphere prevailed. Able seaman Frank Brookshaw, who was aboard the HMS *Anthony*, described the scene:

> To us it was like a birthday party. They were very weak, but I think it was the fact that they had been picked up put new life into them. You'd found something, you'd recovered something, bringing them back from the dead. Within a few hours and certainly by next morning the children were running around.[7]

Undoubtedly the discovery of forty-one adults and six children, eight days after the sinking of the *City of Benares*, lifted the mood of the nation. Newspaper headlines like 'Back from the Dead' recounted the details and drama of the rescue, and Mary Cornish became an overnight heroine. But there were other acts of heroism and self-sacrifice. The Salvation Army highlighted the role played by one of its escorts who was also aboard the *City of Benares*:

> Captain Elma Shaw, a slum department officer, has received from Mr Geoffrey Shakespeare, chairman of the Children's Overseas Reception Board, a letter of thanks for the 'very efficient way you carried out your duty as an escort, and particularly for the way in which you behaved after the ship was torpedoed. The steadiness and bravery you showed and the

leadership you gave the children was undoubtedly one of the main factors in preserving their lives.'[8]

Yet some escorts, such as Father Rory O' Sullivan, discovered that they were not mentally or physically equipped to deal with trauma and experienced mental health breakdowns as a consequence. Members of the rescue ships were also haunted for the remainder of their lives, primarily by the images of those they could not save. Reg Charlton, for instance, described his ordeal and the emotions that engulfed the whole of the crew:

I was on the bridge and the ship slowed down. As we approached we looked around, and it was the most grim and heartbreaking scene. There were boats half filled with water. It was difficult to take it all in at once, but then in particular I saw lifeboats that had children – dead children. Then when the ship came closer, we saw the detail. There was a boat – three quarters full of water – that had a man sitting in the bows and he was up to his chest in water, but he was holding up a boy and had his hand under the boy's chin to keep it clear of water. Whether he was alive or the boy was alive, I don't know. It was a cruel sight to see. The next little boat I looked at had a girl, a little girl, maybe eight or nine, and she was face down with her hair floating out in the water and that was a distressing thing. I was very, very touched to see that girl, with her beautiful hair all floating. That image was heartbreaking. That's what still lives with me to this day. The image of little ones and the why – imagining what had happened.

Then I saw another lifeboat that seemed to have some more children in, but at that point I had to leave the bridge to go down to help with the nets. We were throwing scrambling nets over the side and then helping people come alongside and hold them. They got their little boats up to the side of the ship, and the captain manoeuvred the ship alongside. Then I went to the gangway which had been got down a few feet into the water and I had two or three sailors with me to hand people up the steps. They were mainly women first, I think there were about three or four women, and these ladies had been working the oars when they came alongside the ship. In the bows there were a few lascar seamen, who had also survived. But we were hearing horrific stories of the way the lifeboats had tipped out from the davits when they had tried to lower them into the sea. That's where many of the crew and passengers died – a cold death for those people who had gone into the sea when the lifeboat launch didn't work properly. But of all the images, the one that will never leave me was seeing the lifeboats with dead children in, at least two girls in different lifeboats and the man holding up a boy in the flooded lifeboat. I will always think of the little girls with their hair drifting, floating in a fan on the water. The impact on me, so sad and distressing it was. I felt heartbroken. Everybody felt the same, terribly emotional and distressed. We all felt awful. We all of us went through that whole range – that whole gamut of emotions of anger, rage and distress. Some of the crew definitely wept when they saw it all. I remember that we all felt tearful indeed. It was such a horrendous thought when we saw what was left of them, in the life boats, and what obviously happened to them. It was knowing in your mind what they had gone through, the image of what was happening to them when we were steaming towards them. Well, our worst imaginings had been realised when we thought of this dastardly death the people had suffered. But it was helpful in a way to our spirits that we'd saved some, that we were there to rescue some people.[9]

Frank Brookshaw was present at the burials of those children who did not survive: 'The Captain read the burial service. The little bodies, wrapped in sailcloth covered with a Union flag, were committed to the deep. It was an experience I will never forget.'[10]

Yet amid the sorrow and tragic scenes there were amazing acts of courage and heroism. There were incidences whereby adults sacrificed their own lives in order that children could live, and cases where younger children had survived simply because their older siblings had given them their own life jackets. Some children had realised the seriousness of the situation and had demonstrated great gallantry, such as Colin Ryder Richardson, who was awarded the king's award for bravery. His memory of his survival and the fate of others who were not so lucky remained with him sixty-five years after the event:

I still have constant nightmares, it's very difficult. These days people go into various forms of therapy, but in 1940 these kinds of things were not thought of. The attitude was: its tough luck, now get on with your life. Probably at the time it seemed right and reasonable, but many people who suffered these experiences clearly needed more. I've read quite a lot about this since, and found that other people in these sorts of situations take it in a similar way. They may be a hero at the time, but afterwards they find they are very reluctant to talk about it. When you are through it, the distress of the whole event becomes just too much. I have nightmares when I wake up screaming and I'm just back on the lifeboat or back on the ship, back into some part of the story. They have that saying, 'Lest we forget' – well you don't forget, you never forget.[11]

In addition to acts of heroism, many of the surviving children afloat in the lifeboats could recall the kindness and protectiveness afforded to them by the mainly lascar *City of Benares* crew. They gave their food and water rations to the children and were much weaker than other survivors as a consequence. Before the war the *City of Benares* had travelled between Bombay and Great Britain; when the ship was torpedoed, most of the lascar crew were attired in thin cotton clothing, which was suited to the climate in Bombay but not to the colder and harsher elements of the North Atlantic Ocean. A few lascars managed to grab overcoats or blankets as they scuttled towards the lifeboats, but most had only the clothing they stood up in. As a result of their inade-quate clothing many of the lascars were found to be suffering from exposure by the time they were rescued, and many later died and were buried at sea.

In the wake of the *City of Benares* tragedy, a distraught Geoffrey Shakespeare attempted to inform all parents of the disaster. To this end he trudged the streets of London, Glasgow and Liverpool knocking on their doors and breaking the dreadful news as gently as possible. However, there was much confusion with regard to the identification of the children who had perished, and since many children were rescued up to ten days after the sinking, some parents were given false information. Subsequently there were immense and delightful reunions when children who were thought to have died turned up again, alive and reasonably well. Parents who had been told that there was no hope because their children were missing at sea, presumed dead, were suddenly on the receiving end of the best phone calls imaginable. As one female survivor recalled:

At first, I was a bit overwhelmed at seeing my mum, but she was there, and it was such a relief. It was like a shining light to me to see my mother, because she was the one person ... I was just overcome actually, but she was overcome too. She cried a bit, but she was very sensitive too. My mother always was actually, and she just hugged me. We kissed each other and that was how it went. We were thrilled, thrilled to be with each other again. I think that all I said was 'Oh Mum,' I think that was it, 'Oh Mum I love you.' I think it was that sort of thing and she hugged me. She said 'Oh, thank goodness,' she said, 'Thank God you're home.' And that was the way it was.[12]

Reunions also took place aboard the rescue ships. Cypher Officer John Collins was aboard HMS *Hurricane* and took part in the rescue operation:

About midnight on 17th September I unscrambled a signal from the Admiralty commanding the *Hurricane* to go to a position in the North Atlantic where survivors had been reported. We hoped to lower the whaler to go off and pick them up. All the survivors we picked up were severely dehydrated, shocked and emotionally upset. Three little boys, aged about seven, could not be revived. One little boy being shown around the ship saw his sister's dressing gown hanging up to dry and he thought she had been drowned, there was a monumental reunion![13]

Amidst the ongoing drama of rescues, chaos, loss and confusion, one thing was certain – the fate of the *City of Benares*, its victims and survivors, signalled the end of government endorsement of the overseas evacuation of children. In the weeks that followed the disaster, Geoffrey Shakespeare informed the national press that the CORB scheme had been suspended to allow an official inquiry to take place. Shakespeare argued that speedier ships, staffed entirely by an English crew, would ensure that children travelling abroad reached their destinations, but his colleagues at Whitehall and the Prime Minister Winston Churchill were not convinced. Three months after the sinking of the *City of Benares* he informed his colleagues in the House of Commons that 'In present conditions it is obviously undesirable to resume evacuation of children overseas, but as soon as circumstances permit, a further statement will be made.'[14]

An official inquiry into the *City of Benares* disaster discovered that the ship was carrying too many passengers and there were not enough lifeboats. Adult survivors reported that there were language barriers with the 166 Lascar members of the crew and they did not understand the English captain when he issued his abandon ship orders at the time of the disaster. Lascars also failed to implement rescue procedures effectively. In addition to this fundamental problem, there were also rumours of a clash of personalities between Captain Nicholls of the *City of Benares* and Admiral Mackinnon, the Commander of the convoy. Indeed, the latter ignored Admiralty instructions to disperse the convoy at noon on the 17 September and kept the convoy travelling at a very slow speed, even when it was clear that Naval protection had ceased. It was impossible for the inquiry to discern the reasoning behind these actions, however, because Admiral Mackinnon died as a result of the tragedy.[15]

The inquiry concluded that the disaster occurred because of the lack of adequate naval protection and the incompetence of the Lascar crew.

Attempts to resurrect the CORB scheme continued until March 1941, but no one was prepared to risk another catastrophe. Children continued to be evacuated overseas by private arrangement, and by American-led initiatives, but British government CORB schemes were officially shelved. The CORB advisory committee and administration continued to exist with a drastically reduced staff, in order to monitor those children who had managed to arrive at their destinations and to prepare for their return journeys once hostilities had ceased. The 200,000 mothers and children who were still on the government waiting list for overseas evacuation were briskly informed of the demise of the CORB scheme.

Before the government pulled the plug on CORB, a total of 2,863 British children had arrived in the Dominions under its auspices. Canada received 1,532, Australia 577, South Africa 353 and New Zealand 202 children. No children were sent to the United States of America under the scheme, but 838 were sent under the auspices of the American Committee for the Evacuation of European Children with the collaboration of CORB.[16] However, these figures are highly misleading in terms of the actual numbers of sea-vacs, and they represent only a fraction of the number of British children who set sail for foreign shores between 1939 and 1945. It is estimated that somewhere between 13,000 and 20,000 children were relocated overseas for the duration of the war. Accurate figures are not available, because many records were destroyed by bomb damage, and because a large number of children were sent abroad during emergency situations with only scant documentation.

Nevertheless, children evacuated via the CORB scheme experienced far less class conflict than their domestic counterparts, although the fact that greater stress was placed on national identity rather than on social class did not totally eliminate class conflict. In some instances there were the more familiar problems of home sickness and differences in standards of living caused problems for some children. But only a few failed completely to adjust to their new lives. The scheme benefited from the fact that 63 per cent of CORB children actually went to live with relatives or friends recommended by their parents. The remaining number mirrored the problems that were associated with domestic evacuation, in that 30 per cent were removed from their original host families and only 7 per cent were successfully placed in one home for the duration of the war. Yet nearly all CORB children were placed in homes of a higher social class than their own, and consequently received far better health and educational opportunities as a result. But the sinking of the SS *City of Benares* had the knock-on effect of sinking CORB objectives, and dramatically ended Shakespeare's dream of offering more children a safe haven overseas. Speaking in 1942, he stoutly defended the work and achievements of CORB and claimed that children evacuated overseas had been provided with a stable environment, continuity with regard to health and education and immeasurable safety, predicting that 'the international children will be, if anything, ahead of the 'domestics' because of the broadening experiences made possible by their travels'.[17]

Shakespeare's words were far-sighted, and research has since confirmed his opinion in this regard. The oral history testimonies of ex-CORB evacuees reveals that at least 75 per cent took advantage of their new opportunities. Subsequently they ascended the social ladders in their adoptive countries with relative ease, and children evacuated via the CORB scheme discovered that their lives were enriched by a profoundly positive and transformative experience. Even those sea-vacs who suffered emotionally and psychologically stilled fared better in the long run than the British children who stayed behind to face the Blitz.[18]

But whatever the merits of overseas evacuation, the risks involved in sending British children overseas as part of an official government initiative were, after the sinking of the *City of Benares*, too great to contemplate. The majority of British government ministers decided that, regardless of whether it was viewed as a political manoeuvre or as a humanitarian gesture, the risks far outweighed any potential advantages to the children concerned. As Shakespeare recalled:

> It was clear that the German submarine menace had now become such that it would be unsafe to continue the evacuation scheme. I so advised the War Cabinet, and it was immediately decided to suspend it. On the morning after this disaster my first thought was to disembark all the children who might have embarked on other ships sailing for the Dominions. I telephoned to Glasgow and six hundred children, bitterly disappointed, and many of them in tears, were landed at the last moment. One of the ships from which they had disembarked was torpedoed and sunk within twelve hours of sailing. I thanked God for his mercy that the children were safe on shore.[19]

The heartfelt sentiments of those aboard the SS *City of Benares* were summed up in a poem written by Hugh Simms:

> A cold grey sea and a cold grey mist
> Are kissing little children that their mothers kissed
> Think on it my England ever shall you live
> But never, never, must the sea or you forgive.[20]

Notes

1   'Diabology', *British Journal of Education*, 27 September 1940, vol. LXXVI no. (1968) p. 211.
2   Lord Quinton, oral history testimony, BBC interview July 1999.
3   Bess Cummings, oral history testimony, BBC interview July 1999.
4   Lord Quinton, oral history testimony, BBC interview July 1999.
5   *Ibid*.
6   Huxley, E., *Atlantic Ordeal: The Story of Mary Cornish* (1941).

7   Frank Brookshaw, oral history testimony, BBC interview July 1999.
8   Salvation Army, *War Cry*, 28 September 1940, quoted in Parsons, M. & Starns, P. *The Evacuation: The True Story* (1999) p. 136.
9   Menzies, J., *Children of the Doomed Voyage* (2005) pp. 134–5.
10 Frank Brookshaw, oral history testimony, BBC interview July 1999.
11 Menzies, J., *Children of the Doomed Voyage* (2005) pp. 190–1.
12 *Ibid* p. 187.
13 John Collins, oral history testimony, July 1999.
14 Hansard House of Commons Parliamentary Debates 5th Series written answers by Geoffrey Shakespeare, 21 January 1941, col. 70–1.
15 For a more in-depth look at the issues surrounding the SS *City of Benares* please examine the Dominion papers and CORB documents that are housed in the National Archive, beginning with PRO DO131/43.
16 Hansard House of Commons Parliamentary Debates 5th Series oral answers, Geoffrey Shakespeare speaking with regard to CORB, 25 February 1941, col. 374.
17 Geoffrey Shakespeare speaking to members of the Pilgrim Club at Grosvenor House, 17 February 1942.
18 Lin, P., 'National Identity and Social Mobility: Class, Empire and the British Government Overseas Evacuation of Children during the Second World War', *Twentieth Century British History* vol. 7 no. 3, (1996) p. 333. For more information about children and the Blitz please see Starns, P., *Blitz Families: The Children Who Stayed Behind* (2012).
19 Shakespeare, G., *Let Candles Be Brought In* (1949) p. 274.
20 Johnson, D.E., *Exodus of Children: Story of the Evacuation 1939–45* (1985) p. 120.

5

American Resolve

It was somewhat ironic, and in some quarters embarrassing, given the negative ministerial views of American mothers that had been bandied about within the House of Commons, that American generosity towards British children knew no bounds. Moreover, by the summer of 1940 the American people had volunteered in their thousands to provide a safe haven for British children. Significantly, most of these offers appeared to be unconditional. American politicians attempted to establish a mercy ship scheme, and Mr Eric Biddle, Director of the United States Committee for the Care of European Children, stated that his government were prepared to send the ships as far as Ireland to pick up British children. But this measure relied entirely on a guarantee of safe passage from the Germans. Not surprisingly, British politicians were not about to rely on the Germans for anything, let alone the safety of British children. But the American press continued to whip up enthusiasm for an evacuation scheme. The *New York Times* declared:

> The United States of America want children of all classes and the cities request that the British government send all that they can.
>
> The suggestion that so far only children of titled and wealthy Britons have been evacuated to the United States is strongly criticised by the American Committee in London for the evacuation of children. Mr Justin Weddell, chairman of the committee, speaking to a reporter today, blamed exchange restrictions for the fact that the children so far sent have belonged to families who have travelled and have made well-to-do friends in the States. 'We are arranging to take all kinds of children' he said. Cities have said, 'send us all you can – poor or well-to-do.' Some American sponsors are paying for the passage of poorer children.[1]

The movement of British children across to the USA was also encouraged by America's First Lady, Eleanor Roosevelt. By 9 July 1940, Mrs Roosevelt had established the National Child Refugee Committee in an effort to raise the equivalent of £1 million to secure passage and accommodation for British and European children. Furthermore, once Mrs Roosevelt became chairman of the newly established United States Committee for the Care of European Children, offers to host evacuees flooded into their headquarters. An opinion poll suggested that at least 7,000 parents had come forward with offers of help. Mrs Roosevelt was also instrumental in cutting red tape within immigration departments and speeding up the process of evacuation. On 25 July the *New York Times* stated that:

> The U.S. Committee for the Care of European Children (U.C.C.E.C.) announce that London developments have cleared the way for an immediate 'mass migration' of British children, rich and poor alike, to the United States. Cablegrams said that space for a thousand children has been allotted in ships bound for North American ports in the next few weeks. The Committee said a thousand visas have been cleared in Washington and would be issued to London today. British sources have supplied private funds to transport the children, while the U.S. Committee has deposited 50,000 dollars the equivalent of 12,500 pounds required by the United States as an insurance against any of the children becoming public charges. Up to the present the children arriving here have been specific guests of specific persons, but this contingent will be 'unknowns'.[2]

A Reuters News Agency article was even more dramatic, claiming that:

> Hitler may hurl hell towards England at any moment and certainly he will strike soon. America must act instantly. America must say to England 'Our bars are down to your children. Send them by the thousands; it is our duty and privilege to give them a home. There is no conceivable reason for not taking 60,000 children if England wants to send them to the New World and more too.' And let us stand side by side with Canada to relieve her of any part of the burden of providing for children which her war effort might make difficult. British circles in New York consider the United States ready to receive many thousands of children within the next few days either direct or through Canada. In Canada it has been announced that the province of British Columbia alone is prepared to absorb 10,000 children immediately. No fears are entertained here that homes will not be found immediately on this continent for almost unlimited numbers of children.[3]

Faced with such overwhelming hospitality it would have been churlish for the British government to refuse. However, with the demise of the mercy ship scheme they were hard-pressed to get children over to the USA even if they wanted to – although, despite this major obstacle, at least 838 sea-vacs reached America with the assistance of CORB, and thousands more entered because of private arrangements. Many did so under the auspices of American company schemes such as those initiated by Kodak, Ford, Eastman and Hoover. According to the author C. Jackson, there were a number of British government ministers who were prepared to overlook the supposed failings of American mothers and favoured the idea of sending children to the USA in the hope of provoking an international incident that would bring America into the war.[4]

Yet from a British standpoint there is no evidence to support such a con-spiracy theory. In fact, an analysis of parliamentary papers reveals that the majority of British ministers continued to prefer evacuation schemes that sent children to the Dominions, although Winston Churchill did indicate that American ships in British ports would have been a welcome sight, stat-ing 'If a movement to send United States ships to these shores were to set foot from the other side of the Atlantic, it would immediately engage the most earnest attention of His Majesty's Government.'[5]

Nevertheless, American Congressmen did express their own suspi-cions, openly suggesting that Britain might well consider using children as a means to provoke an incident and urging caution in this respect. These unfounded suspicions naturally served to sour Anglo-American relation-ships. Mrs Roosevelt toed the Congress line and was explicit in expressing her concerns. When asked in the summer of 1940 whether it was possible to transport children by using American Red Cross ships she was adamant: 'It would be a very grave responsibility, and might get us into the war. The USA in all probability would not feel that they could assume that responsibility.'[6]

Whilst the lack of mercy ships and American Red Cross ships hampered the evacuation of children to the USA to a degree, over 10,000 British chil-dren were taken in by American families between 1939 and 1941. Such children did not prompt America to join the war, but to the obvious delight of British ministers they did tug at the heartstrings of the American public. Announcing the arrival of British children in Canton, sponsored by the Hoover vacuum cleaner company, the journalist Lois Zimmer published an open letter in the Canton Repository entitled 'Dear British Parents':

> It was that little group of 'in-betweens' who wrung our hearts. Too old to be treated as babies, and too young to realise what it was all about, they walked off the train like soldiers, looking neither to the left nor right.

Small girls carried their best-loved dolls and little boys swung duffle bags in an effort at nonchalance, or clutched a newly acquired souvenir, perhaps a 'dead' flash bulb or a stick of gum.

It's hard to express that feeling that moved so many of those onlookers to unashamed tears. It's as if each one had been trying to see your child for you, rather than for himself. They knew your love, your pride in your child's courage and your relief in his safety. Each was conscious that there was something holy in being entrusted with the care of a stranger's child; that it symbolized the parents' unquestioning faith and selfless courage.[7]

Upon their arrival British children were placed either in families that had been previously nominated by their parents, or in suitably vetted and approved host families. Great care had been taken to provide children with loving families, but placements were not infallible. Strangely, most problems arose within the nominated families. For instance one young girl was placed with an aunt who turned out to be a brothel madam. There were others who found themselves living with families with whom their parents had only established a minor acquaintance and who upon arrival were found to be totally unsuitable. These were often children who had been placed with elderly persons or those who were suffering from chronic sickness. Such families had the best of intentions but were not capable of caring for lively young children. Consequently these children were rehoused.

Guest children were in fact, scattered across the United States, but there were three areas where the residents were more welcoming than others. These were New York, Massachusetts and Ohio. Inhabitants of New York were renowned for their philanthropy and for offering help on an international scale, Massachusetts had a long colonial history and displayed a pro-British political stance and citizens of industrial Ohio were deeply respectful of the hard-working British people who lived and worked alongside them.[8]

Yet the enthusiastic rhetoric of the American press and the fervour with which ordinary Americans offered their services to all British children was completely at odds with existing immigration legislation. Even with the assistance of Mrs Roosevelt, persistent obstacles to the mass immigration of British and European children remained. Geoffrey Shakespeare woefully wrote:

Parents were given the option of sending their children to the United States of America and about thirty thousand applicants were received. It was disappointing that an official scheme of evacuation to the USA never operated. In the early stages I had seen Mr Kennedy, the American Ambassador, and the details of the scheme were subsequently worked out in Washington, but the rigid form of the American immigration laws presented many obstacles. There were difficulties about migrants whose passages had been paid. There was a quota scheme applicable to each nationality, and too many immigrants from Britain would have upset the quota.[9]

Furthermore, the seemingly unconditional offers were, in fact, illusory, as Shakespeare acknowledged:

> Sponsors had to be found to give financial guarantees. The medical tests for migrants were very strict and never could have been applied to children in war time. Moreover, each state in the USA had its own legal code of child welfare and there were many varieties in the different states. The problem of guardianship loomed large. What would happen if a child was dying and the consent of the parents in Britain could not be obtained in time? It is quite erroneous to believe that red tape is the prerogative of the British bureaucrat. All these difficulties had to be resolved and it took time. Throughout the United States the idea of receiving and giving shelter to European children evoked tremendous interest and enthusiasm. It was a typical example of the instantaneous appeal which a humanitarian cause makes to the warm heart of the great republic. Local committees were formed all over the United States and large funds were raised, and the names of prospective hosts and hostesses collected. We had nearly resolved the remaining difficulty when the CORB scheme came to a tragic end in October, as a result of the sinking of the SS *City of Benares* and the worsening of the shipping position in the Atlantic.[10]

Thus British children did not travel to the United States as part of the CORB scheme. They did however, travel to American shores under the aegis of a 'semi-official' American scheme that was established by Mr Lawrence Tweedy, the chairman of the American Chamber of Commerce. Indeed, a number of Anglo-American causes were implemented as a result of Mr Tweedy's efforts. He became the chairman of the American Committee for the Care of European Children in London and was instrumental in assisting the evacuation of British children to America via a number of big private company schemes.

Mr Herbert Hoover, head of the famous vacuum cleaner company, for example, paid all the passages for children of his British employees. The British managing director of Hoover Ltd in London, Mr Colston, also took it upon himself to write a letter to these children, copies of which were given to them before their departure stating:

Now a lot of things I have written here, I wrote to three children a few weeks ago. Could you guess who? They are my own three children. Their names are Jenn aged ten, Ian aged six and Colin aged three. And why do you think I wrote to them? Because they were leaving for America as you are and they are now in Canton, Ohio, where Mr Hoover lives and where you are going to, and they will be pleased when a lot more British children arrive. Won't that be fun?

One more thing, every now and again – and on the boat too if possible – if you are old enough to write yourself, just send your Mummy and Daddy a little note because they will be ever so pleased and happy when they get it.

I want you to have a lovely time and I want you always to behave like your Mummy and Daddy would want you to behave and just like you do when you are trying your best to be good. You are all Britishers and when you arrive, and all the time you are away I want the Americans to say, 'Aren't these British children nice? They always say please and thank you and they always try to help make everyone very, very happy. I hope you will each help the other and have such a good time together that when you come back you will say, 'Mummy and Daddy, we have had the time of our lives'.[11]

A great number of British children arrived in the USA via the railway network from Canada, particularly those who were destined for New Haven, but substantial numbers of children also arrived on American shores directly from ocean-going liners. Such trips were sporadic and unpredictable and the children were referred to as refugees rather than evacuees. On 4 October 1940 the *New York Times* announced:

The first group of refugee children to come direct to New York in more than a month arrived here yesterday on three British liners, the Cunard White Star liners, *Scythia*, *Samaria* and the Furness cargo passenger liner *Western Prince*. There were more than five hundred children in all, approximately two hundred and fifty each on the two larger vessels and thirty-seven on the *Western Prince*. Although none of the ships' officers would discuss their voyage in detail, it was evident from the talk of the less inhibited youngsters that the three vessels had come most of the way in convoy, probably the same one.[12]

In addition to the evacuation schemes established by big American companies, more elitist schemes were introduced by certain universities such as Yale, Harvard and Rhodes. Scholars and alumni of these educational institutions were asked if they could house one or more children of Oxbridge dons. Again, there was an undercurrent of eugenic thought in these arrangements, a notion that children of the intelligentsia were in some way more important than other children. This somewhat sinister agenda, however, did not seem to influence the children of academics. They settled down quickly in their new environments, and in such cases Americans usually acted *in loco parentis*, since the majority of guest children were unaccompanied. The chief archivist for Yale explained:

> The majority of the Yale hosts were faculty. Among them were the eminent English Professor Maynard Mack; Robert Dudley French, master of Jonathan Edwards College; and Edith Jackson, a pioneer of psychoanalysis and child psychology. There was no lack of funds. The evacuees' families, as well as two foundations, contributed more than a hundred thousand dollars.[13]

Across the board the majority of British children who resided in America for the duration of war did so within affluent family networks. Such families had offered assistance and homes for guest children because of a strong sense of altruism. These children were generally treated with kindness, generosity and care. Even those who were initially suffering from severe homesickness eventually thrived within their supportive family frameworks. Furthermore, many of the host families received no financial aid whatsoever and tended their guest children at considerable cost to their own purse. To begin with, funds to support British children had been sent to host families via private arrangement or through agencies working for the British government, but once the Battle of Britain had reached its peak in September 1940, Winston Churchill placed an embargo on all funds, private or otherwise, leaving the country. Without warning, therefore, families in America and the Dominions who had been in receipt of money which in some way contributed to the upkeep of British children, were suddenly devoid of all income.

It should also be noted that American welfare systems did not adequately support evacuee or native children in any shape or form. Welfare systems generally were very sporadic and child welfare programmes did not exist in many small towns and rural areas. Between 1940 and 1945 it was possible to find small children at home alone and huddled inside locked parked vehicles, abandoned for hours because their mothers were employed full-time within industrial centres. The problem was particularly acute for mothers with children under 2 years old. The Children's Bureau organised a conference to discuss approaches to childcare. The Conference on Day Care for Working Mothers concluded that 'during a period when the work of women is necessary there is a public responsibility to provide adequate child care which should include a network of nursery provision and basic community services for children'. However, it was not until 1944 that principles for childcare were agreed across the states as follows:

- Decisions as to the care of young children must be made in the light of a child's needs.
- Every effort must be made to preserve for the baby his right to have care from his mother.
- Advisory and counselling services should be a part of every programme of child care.
- Foster family day care needs to meet the baby's needs rather than group care.
- Group care is not a satisfactory method of caring for children under two years of age.
- Whenever possible the age of admission to group care should be fixed at between two and three years of age.[14]

This agreement, approved by all childcare organisations, did not automatically improve child welfare and it was some time before recommendations were implemented. Hosts in charge of evacuee children therefore needed to apply considerable diligence in caring for their small charges, and they were often out of pocket because they were required to pay their medical bills without any assistance from British parents. There is no evidence, however, that a lack of British-generated funds resulted in any resentment towards evacuees. Some families were forced to tighten their belts but nevertheless resolved to see the job through for the duration. For their part, most of the evacuees appeared to be acutely aware of their role as British ambassadors but, simultaneously, those who resided in America entered into the spirit and culture of their new surroundings with enthusiasm and vigour. Adam Raphael, for example, was one such evacuee. He fell in love with Princeton and recalled a particularly amusing incident:

I look back on Princeton with delight. It had woods and streams where you could play, and right outside my house was a hill where I learned to ride a bike. My best friend Skipper was across the road and I just became an American child. My sister had been skating at the local skating rink and she came back very excited and said 'Mum I've found somebody to help with my maths homework.' Mum asked who it was. My sister replied that 'He was a very nice elderly gentleman who said he would help me.' Mother said cautiously 'You had better bring him home to tea.' Anyway, she brought him back to tea and it turned out that the elderly gentleman was Einstein![15]

Incidents such as these were widespread and it seemed to the guest children that America was truly a land of promise and adventure. Furthermore, many of them were deliberately shielded from the harsh realities of the war. Some criticism of elitist evacuation schemes remained, particularly those associated with the intelligentsia. However, there were cases where such elitism appeared to be justified. Vera Brittain for instance, author of the First World War manuscript *The Testament of Youth* had been informed that her name and the names of her family members were on a Gestapo blacklist and therefore the risk to her children was heightened. As a mother of two children, Brittain ensured that her son and daughter were sent to America by private arrangement. Indeed, Brittain's daughter, Baroness Shirley Williams, was one of a small minority of guest children who were intent on following every detail of the war and all the events that were affecting her homeland. Recalling her time in America, the Baroness stated that:

> Letters from home were always a bit delayed and late. Newspapers with a couple of pages about the war, usually covering both the German and the British side equally ... but then the Battle of Britain tended to produce some sympathy because we were the defenders so there was a lot about the Battle of Britain and there were lots of films ... I used to go and watch the R.K.O., the weekly films about the news and so one caught up with quite a lot with that. I guess it wasn't too difficult to follow in a very broad sense what was happening, and again I was lucky enough to be with a politically very interested family so that they wanted to know about what was happening in the war as much as I did.[16]

Yet whether or not guest children in America followed the news in detail or not they were all acutely aware that the situation facing their homeland was serious. The American public had affectionately nicknamed the evacuees 'Britishers' and Britain's success in winning the Battle of Britain was greeted with an enormous sense of public relief, and later, when America joined the war following the Japanese attack on Pearl Harbor on the 7 December 1941, there was a growing sense of camaraderie between the young Britishers and their American hosts. Before this event the generous resolve of the American public was always at odds with members of the American Congress, who were fearful that an ocean voyage catastrophe would jeopardise American neutrality, whereas after the Pearl Harbor attack an emerging sense of wartime solidarity did much to reinforce the special relationship that already existed between Britain and America. Furthermore, although American resolve to offer a safe haven for 60,000 British children did not materialise, the children who did reach American shores were undoubtedly afforded social, educational and cultural opportunities that were far superior to those being offered to the children who had remained in Britain.

Notes

1   *New York Times*, 6 July 1940.
2   *New York Times*, 25 July 1940.
3   Reuters News Agency, 10 June 1940.
4   Jackson, C., *Who Will Take Our Children?* (1985) ch. 3–6.
5   Gilbert, M. (ed.), *The Churchill War Papers* vol. 2 p. 542.
6   Reuters News Agency, 1940
7   Zimmer, L. 'Dear British Parents', *The Canton Repository*, 22 August 1940.
8   Inglis, R. *The Children's War* (1989) p. 123.
9   Shakespeare, G., *Let Candles Be Brought In* (1949) p. 251.
10 *Ibid.* p. 251–2.
11 Manful, H., 'Hoover Evacuees, Part One: A Haven For Children During World War Two' at *http://www.cantonrep.com/x1688624942/Hoover-Evacuees-Part-1-A-haven-for-children-during-WWII/?tag=2*
12 'British Children Give the Thumbs Up', *New York Times*, 4 October 1940.
13 Schiff, J.A., 'Yale's' Foster Children' (2010) at *www.yalealumnimagazine.com/issues/2010_07/old yale267*.
14 United States of America records of the Children's Bureau 1940–45.
15 Raphael, A., oral history testimony, BBC interview July 1999, quoted in M. Parsons & P. Starns, *The Evacuation: The True Story* (1999) p. 166.
16 *Ibid.* p. 158–9.

6

Voyages

As British children began their journeys to foreign shores, very few of them were aware that they stood on the brink of an exciting adventure. Most of them had only travelled a few hundred yards from their homes prior to the point of embarkation. Huddled together on the quayside like little bundles of energy, the children clutched their jam-packed bags and a toy. Their meagre luggage contained an assortment of clothes and utensils that would hopefully see them through their voyage and beyond. Boys carried one suit, one warm coat, a mackintosh, a long-sleeved pullover, a pair of khaki shorts and knickers, two flannel shirts, one Panama hat, one pair of flannel shorts, two sets of pyjamas, one pair of boots or shoes, one pair of sandals or plimsolls, six handkerchiefs, two towels and a comb. Girls carried some similar general items such as shoes, sandals and underwear, but also three cotton dresses, two cardigans, a hairbrush, toothpaste and a toothbrush. Aboard ship they were encouraged to keep diaries to record their observations, thoughts and feelings, and they were taught basic information about the culture and history of their destination countries. Alongside the regular lifeboat drills and safety instructions, physical exercise classes, church services and regular mealtimes, formal lessons and diary writing provided the main structure for a child's day. Furthermore, it is within the pages of surviving diaries that unique insights can be gleaned with regard to individual voyages. These diaries reveal that almost all children experienced homesickness, seasickness and a fear of the unknown. But in addition to these shared experiences children also recorded distinctive individual information. Their drawings in journals were also insightful. For example, as she approached Bombay en route to Australia, a young girl named Marjorie Ursell sketched an outline drawing and wrote the word Bombay in the corner of her picture. The dominant image in the same picture however, was of London's iconic Big Ben, standing proudly amongst the lesser aspects of the drawing. Extracts from Marjorie's diary, which displayed her childhood grasp of grammar and spelling, recorded the day-to-day events and observations aboard ship as follows:

September 11th
I saw a whole school of purpoies.

September 12th
I saw a whale.

September 16th
We sighted Bombay about ten o'clock in the morning we stayed in the harbour all the night, not in the docks. I went on the sun deck with the section and it was beautiful, we are expecting to go ashore tomorrow.

September 17th
Today we pulled into the docks about three o'clock we where told at half past three we would go ashore we had rest hour then got ready to go on land. I haved speaked to the English m.p.s in the army which were on guard, they had been in India for six and a half years and would have been in England if this silly war was not on. In the evening we went for a walk, as we did not get of in the afternoon. But they sent cakes and oranges instead.

September 18th
We went into mid stream again today. We did nothing exciting this afternoon but stayed on deck. In the evening there was a great storm with no rain it thundered and the lightning was terrific. It lightened up the sky.

September 19th
The day past quickly. In the evening we had pictures.

September 20th
We went back into harbour again. We got off at about two o'clock in buses and went for two (and more) hours ride, then we stoped after a long ride around Bombay. We had a bottle of lemonade fizz each, 1 bun, 1 cake and 2 tarts. When we where on bus going back we had three sweets each. The shops are open and some are just stools in a square. The men dressed according to their religion. The ladys also did the same, some where covered completely.

September 21st
We left Bombay and did nothing all day.

September 22nd & 23rd
We where on the sea making way to Ceylon.

September 24th
We sited Colambo this morning, this afternoon we got of in little boats to
the shore we where taken in threes and fours with different ladys in cars
to the zoo. There we had tea and ice cream. After that we look around the
zoo with beautiful flowers and animals. After looking round we went back
by car to the docks again and into little boats back to the ship, and then to
back as it was 8 o'clock.

September 25th
To-day we stayed on board, while the private passengers and escourts got
of it was dismalest all day, this afternoon we moved.

September 26th to 30th
All these days we have been at sea. Tomorrow we expect to reach Singapore.

October 1st
Today at 9 o'clock we went out to a school where we played about with the
girls at the school, there was 5 different countrys in the class we went to
Indian, Persian, Malya Jappanes and English. We had dinner there, after
that we went in bus for a ride then back to ship with a bottle of fizz.[1]

Alongside the mundane daily routines, children recorded unusual moments,
and scenes of breathtaking beauty. Whilst aboard the *Duchess of Atholl* for
example, en route to America, Baroness Williams recalled:

We took a long time to make the crossing, fourteen days I think it was.
We went right up through the icebergs in an attempt to shake off the
submarines. I remember waking up one morning, very early, dawn, five
o' clock in the morning and looking out of the porthole and seeing what
appeared to be, not more than maybe thirty yards away, an iceberg,
fantastic and absolutely beautiful beyond belief, with the early morning
sun shining on it. It was completely iridescent, pink, blue and green and
every colour one could imagine because it was reflecting the prism and
I was absolutely enraptured.[2]

Others remembered the electric atmosphere on board ship at noteworthy moments. For instance, as a young girl on her way to South Africa, Barbara Browne remembered, 'There was excitement especially when we saw Table Mountain.'[3]

Whereas Margaret Wood stated, 'I remember the flying fish and crossing the equator. Seeing Cape Town lit up at night, that was a joy.'[4]

Nearly all of the ships when crossing the equator marked the event with celebrations and traditional ceremonies. A young boy en route to South Africa recorded this momentous occasion in his journal:

> Today we pass over the Equator Line and the sun will be immediately above us. At 7.30 a.m. I had a hair cut, which I needed very much. I don't have to pay for the hair cut. I went to breakfast feeling hungry. After that I helped our table steward 'Wally' to clear away. Then I went down to medical inspection. While we were having dinner the Captain came down for dinner and he had a telegram saying 'Father Neptune would come aboard ship and see us. This ceremony is because of our ship crossing the equator. Tea eventually came and while we were having the same, Father Neptune came down and spoke to us. Really it was our doctor, who had put on a beard about 1½ yards long! He handed out slips of paper to say we had crossed the line.[5]

The captain and crew on board all ships carrying children made every effort to make them welcome and to keep them safe, well and entertained. Nevertheless, they remained vigilant and exercised caution at all times throughout their voyages. Miss Jean Johnson, a headmistress from Glasgow, was chief escort on board the SS *Ruahine*, the first ship to carry British children to New Zealand. When recording her memoirs she also highlighted the precautions that were deployed by captain and crew:

> For the first five days life jackets were constantly worn and boat drill was the order of the day. Children became very proficient. On board were twenty five Dutch sailors, 1 captain and officers going out to Curacas to man a German vessel (captured). They were a great asset and helped the children in every way. Very entertaining too, but had harrowing tales to tell of their homeland tragedies.
>
> Third day at dawn we sighted a boat load of survivors being picked up by our convoy. Details of such happenings were withheld from us and rightly too. Captain and officers are never at table and never have their clothes off. We changed course, fourth day – weather bitterly cold. We still had the protection of the Atlantic patrol. Our ship moved in the direct centre of

One boy in our cabin has been sick three times and the other eight times, twice in the cabin. Another boy in another cabin has been sick sixteen times!![9]

Further on in his diary the same lad triumphantly recorded that:

About a fortnight ago everyone was sea-sick but not ME.

I was shown round the kitchen by 'Mr Panto' It was very interesting and he gave me a list of what we eat (200 boys and girls): eggs per week 4,500!!! Potatoes per day: 800cwts!!! Butter per day: 22lbs! Jam and marmalade: 56lbs a day! Salad: beetroot and onion, 25lbs beetroot and 12 onions! Sugar per day 40lbs, tea per day 5lbs!! Cocoa: per day 7lbs. I think it's marvellous what 200 children can eat!!!!![10]

Apart from his preoccupation with food and the fact that he managed to keep it down, this young boy was quite critical about his voyage. In addition to noting that his ship was quite old and had clearly seen better days, he also criticised the size of his cabin, and the fact that he was required to share with other boys. He was unhappy about his daily medical inspections and the fact that his ships' purser refused to hand over any pocket money. His greatest complaint, however, was the fact that his camera had been confiscated. For security purposes all cameras were taken by the crew and locked up for the entire voyage, even those that did not have film. Many of the ships, including the *Llanstephan Castle*, were carrying troops in addition to the sea-vacs and the process of dodging landmines and enemy submarines dictated that security was a major concern. Indeed, throughout their voyages children were encouraged to scan the horizon for enemy ships and report any sightings to the Chief Officer. This fact, however, was not usually recorded in diaries. In order to maintain secrecy, escorts had given children some stringent guidelines to follow with regard to writing home. Topics needed to concentrate on the voyages and points of interest in the ever-changing ocean. Therefore, although children's letters to their parents varied in detail, they generally had a common theme. In the main, they focused on food, sea life, church services, crew members they had assisted with menial tasks such as the laying out of dining tables, amusing incidents, ports of call, lessons and entertainment, and the weather. Furthermore, diaries record that as they travelled through tropical climates children were given a daily dose of quinine to combat malaria and clothed in new loose cotton trousers and socks, along with hats and long-sleeved tunics to prevent mosquito bites. Grease was also applied to their wrists and ankles. Daily medical inspections ensured that children were screened for infectious diseases and quarantined if necessary.

Throughout the journeys CORB children received etiquette and elocution lessons as part of their general education. This process was designed to help them mingle with all social classes aboard ship and to prepare them for the receiving families. Yet despite these efforts, there were signs that class conflict still existed on some of the ships. Captain Power, in charge of the *Nestor*, became the children's advocate when he discovered that private passengers aboard his ship were complaining about the CORB presence generally. He gathered the private passengers and the CORB escorts together for a cocktail party where he told the private passengers in no uncertain terms that the children were evacuees not refugees, that they were his main concern and that if anyone was not satisfied, the ship was calling at Cape Town, and they knew what they could do about it;[11] in response to his speech, the private passengers henceforth held their tongues.

As they approached their destinations some incidents seemed to be highly incongruous. A boy describing his first glimpse of African people was amused by both their clothing and demeanour:

September 8th
I got up at six o'clock, went on deck and had a shower. After a good rub down I went back on deck to find a black man in a small canoe paddling around the ship. The black man wore a Bowler hat and a collar and tie!!!!!! Boys were throwing in money and he first took the Bowler hat off, dived in and got the money. Then he put his Bowler hat back on his head. One thing was very amusing, and that was, he kept on singing 'The Lambeth Walk'!!!!! When I came back on deck again after breakfast there were about fifteen canoes round the ship selling mangoes, coconuts, cloth, bananas and monkeys. There was a man who dived for money. The clothing the natives wore was very funny. Some natives had football shirts on. Some had red shirts with white spots, some with gold spots! Some natives had sailor hats on and some had boy's hats on. All at once they were speaking, trying to sell their goods, but as I said before, we were not allowed to buy anything. I enquired the prices of different goods, and the natives would reply eagerly. Some of the natives started throwing mangoes up and I caught one; and I was told to throw it back and then go and wash my hands.[12]

For children who had been at sea for several weeks, the sight of their destination ports prompted a mixture of enthusiasm and bewilderment. They were encouraged to sing loudly to announce their arrival and they were greeted with a barrage of press attention and joyous cheers from the waiting crowds. Miss Johnson, who along with every other escort had compiled a book of statistics relating to the children in her care, described the arrival:

Pilot and Quarantine Officers appeared and we anchored in mid stream. At 2 p.m. on the 27th of September 1940 the ship was thronged with Ministers and officials of the Dominion, who clambered on board and gave the children an uproarious welcome.[13]

The majority of children were collected at ports by host parents who had been previously nominated to take them. Those without nominated parents waited patiently and with some trepidation to be allocated to families. Most of these children were placed with kind and caring host parents, but a few were not so lucky. Sir Martin Gilbert remembered his arrival as a young boy in Canada with clarity:

I've various photographs of us all when we arrived. In the Canadian press, we arrived in Quebec, we were shown with our thumbs up and the caption read 'Just arrived from the Motherland'.

I don't think it was known which family I was going to because I remember having to wait quite a while in Toronto until a family offered to take me in. My mother had managed to scrounge a rather nice fur coat for me and the first thing that happened was this family didn't think the coat was suitable for a boy but would be very suitable for their two year old daughter. I lost my coat on day one and was given instead a wooden Pinocchio which I proceeded to destroy.[14]

The optimistic Meta Maclean and Margaret Osbourne wrote a song aboard ship which summed up their feelings:

From old lands to the new lands,
Come Britons young and free.
With courage true, we come to you
From our homes across the sea.

Our country has taught us each to be
Steadfast brave and true.
Now we are here, with a song of good cheer
To love and be loved by you.[15]

Press coverage initially focussed on the children's travel stories, but journalists continued to hound British children long after their arrival on foreign shores. Journalists were particularly eager to reveal stories that suggested homes were not all they should be in terms of nurturing juveniles. Every effort had been made to place children with families of a similar type to those they had left behind, but occasionally the background information that accompanied a child was severely limited. In such circumstances organisers were required to make an educated guess as to the child's social class, religious affiliations and cultural environment. Journalists were apt to pounce on any hint of disorganisation and produce their own sound-bite version of events. Geoffrey Shakespeare complained bitterly that:

> One disadvantage of organizing a scheme like CORB was that I came in for a lot of publicity. Children are at all times good copy and splendid subjects for photography, and the press was full of charming pictures of children. Both the BBC and the CBC (Canadian Broadcasting Company) arranged entertaining broadcasts of the children at hostels. I myself was a victim of this publicity in a way I disliked. One enterprising journalist referred to me as 'Uncle Geoffrey' and the title stuck in spite of my efforts to stop it.[16]

Nevertheless, Shakespeare welcomed the press attention to a certain extent, since without such media coverage the children would not have been seen as ambassadors for Britain. Nor would they have tugged at the heartstrings of the receiving nations. News articles continued to feature stories of the guest children for the duration of the war, and they served to highlight both the positive and negative aspects of overseas evacuation. These newspaper reports suggested that some children evacuated overseas were placed with unsuitable host parents. Certainly, around 30 per cent of children were rehoused, some on several occasions, between the autumn of 1940 and the spring of 1944.[15] The remaining 70 per cent, however, described the overwhelming warmth of their host families. These welcoming hosts cosseted the sea-vacs, spoiled them and made every effort to help them to adjust to their new surroundings. From the 12ft Canadian snowdrifts to the mango-laden natives of Africa, British children were learning how to deal with the unusual and the unexpected. Furthermore, regardless of their subsequent experiences very few sea-vacs forgot the details of their ocean voyages. The awe-inspiring sights, sounds and smells of the ever fascinating ocean and its inhabitants, the discovery of new scenery, wildlife and foliage, and the process of adjusting to unfamiliar climates and cultures, all combined to form memories that lasted a lifetime.

Notes

1 Diary of M. Ursell, Imperial War Museum ref. 96/55/1.
2 Baroness Shirley Williams, oral history testimony, BBC interview 1999, Parsons, M. & Starns, P., *The Evacuation: The True Story* (1999), p. 138.

3 *Ibid.*, p. 165.
4 *Ibid.*
5 Diary of G.W. Medway, Imperial War Museum ref. 12/23/3.
6 Memoirs of Miss J. Johnson, Imperial War Museum ref. 11082.
7 *Ibid.*
8 *Ibid.*
9 Letter written by G.W. Medway to his parents whilst en route to South Africa, private papers held at the Imperial War Museum ref. 12/23/3.
10 *Ibid.*
11 Fethney, M., *The Absurd and the Brave (1990)* p. 107–8.
12 Letter written by G.W. Medway to his parents whilst en route to South Africa, private papers held at the Imperial War Museum ref. 12/23/3.
13 Memoirs of Miss J. Johnson, Imperial War Museum ref. 11082.
14 Sir Martin Gilbert, oral history testimony, BBC interview 1999, quoted in Parsons, M. & Starns, P., *The Evacuation: The True Story* (1999) p. 166.
15 Stokes, E., *Innocents Abroad* (1994) p. 80.
16 Shakespeare, G., *Let Candles Be Brought In* (1949) p. 266.
17 National Archive, CORB Advisory Council draft memorandum PRO DO/131/4.

1 Cheerful children are pictured as they board trains to be evacuated. (Kent Messenger Newspaper Group)

2 The smiles belie the range of emotions they and their parents must have felt at this time. (Kent Messenger Newspaper Group)

3 The start of the war was a time of intense acitivty, as troops were on the move to defend britain and her empire and children were evacuated to safety. (HMSO)

4 This propaganda image shows a fond farewell between a father and his young daughter.

5 A crowd of evacuee children await onward transit. (HMSO)

6 Evacuees board a ship to begin their journey.

7 Wartime humour poked fun at the logistcal difficulties of preparing so many chidren for evacuation.

8 An intimate shot of evacuees as they prepare to embark upon their adventure.
(IWM)

9 Boarding the train that will carry them on the first leg of their long journey. (IWM)

10 The children were accompanied by adult escorts entrusted with delivering them safely to their destination. (IWM)

11 Each had a gas mask, issued by the government, and luggage packed into whatever bags their parents could find. (Monica B. Morris Archives)

12 The excitement of these evacuees is plain to see, but there are some apprehensive faces hidden in the crowd. (Monica B. Morris Archives)

13 The *Duchess of Atholl*, one of the many boats that carried sea-vacs across the oceans.

14 Built in Triest in 1936, the MS *Batory* wighed 16,000 tons. She departed from Liverpool docks on 6 August 1940, carrying 477 sea-vacs to Australia.

7

Communications

Contrary to popular belief, children who were evacuated overseas usually maintained reasonable contact with their relatives back home. With regard to communication levels overall there is an ongoing misconception that children who were evacuated within the confines of British shores received frequent weekend visits from their parents, whilst children who were evacuated overseas struggled to make contact with their parents. In fact the reverse is true. Fuel shortages, economic constraints and war work commitments in Britain prevented many city parents from visiting their children who were living in the rural areas. Some could not even manage monthly visits, let alone frequent weekend jaunts to the countryside. Official government policy also dictated communication systems, or the lack of them. For instance, for those involved in the domestic evacuation scheme, advice was abrupt and harsh. City-based mothers were told by government officials to resist getting in touch with their evacuated children because it would prevent them from settling down in the country. Standard letters were written by city children in rural schools reassuring their parents that they were safe and well. All letters were censored and city parents were given no indication that their children may be suffering from homesickness or loneliness. Not surprisingly, many of these children experienced a strong sense of abandonment. Furthermore, it can be argued that government reluctance to support family communications was to some extent responsible for the failure of domestic evacuation. Consequently, 90 per cent of evacuated children were back in British cities by December 1939, and despite subsequent waves of evacuation, the numbers of children living in cities throughout the war continued to exceed those who were living in the countryside.[1]

In comparison, parents of children evacuated overseas were encouraged to maintain frequent contact with their offspring. Indeed, communication networks were an integral part of overseas evacuation schemes, and diligent efforts were made to maintain familial links. Letter- and journal-writing was fundamental to this process, and children started to write to their parents almost as soon as the ships were at sea. A few children wrote very brief notes – 'I am somewhere at sea and food is good.' – while the more conscientious wrote long-winded and detailed missives. Regardless of their writing skills, however, British children who were evacuated under the CORB scheme were expected to maintain regular contact with their parents, and the communications ethos that pervaded overseas evacuation was radically different to the domestic approach. This marked difference in policy was primarily the result of principles and strategic communication plans that were initiated and implemented by Geoffrey Shakespeare. He strongly believed that interaction between children and their relatives was crucial to the scheme's success. The escorts also set the children an example by writing their own detailed letters to their relatives. A letter written in August 1940 by Miss Fleming, an escort aboard the SS *Bayano*, summarised her initial observations:

Here we all are, all aboard at last – poor children, rich children; tall children, small children; shy children, gay children; quiet children, noisy children – diverse by nature but united by circumstance into one large happy family. For some it is the land of dreams come true – they are really sailing in a fine big ship – for all it is a great adventure into the unknown. Boys are already wondering if they can climb up the mast or down the wall decks but unfortunately for them – though fortunately for our peace of mind! – that is not allowed. Girls explore to find some corners for their various plays. They find a piano and soon have it opened. One girl plays while the others gather round to sing. Here and there are groups of boys, one lot finding out the secrets of the ship's inside, another arguing about the different types of ships in the convoy.

Some children amuse themselves with games, other prefer to walk round the decks seeing all there is to see. There always seems to be something interesting happening on a ship. During the evening quieter amusement is sought. Perhaps the chief escort will show us some films – or did someone mention a concert? No lack of talent here! Shy at first but, shyness overcome, many volunteers soon come forward. Our favourite song is a round 'We are Sailing in a big ship' composed by one of our escorts, which causes the ship's timbers to shake.

Has it been said that modern children cannot amuse themselves? Our charges not only amuse themselves but also the ship's company. I expect you are wondering what the escorts are doing in the meantime. Well, they are always somewhere about – one joining in a game, one 'on guard' to see that no venturesome child climbs the rails, etc., one telling stories to the 'babes', and perhaps another doing physical jerks. During meals we are on duty to help the little ones and also explain the mysteries of the array of cutlery! Bed time comes and the babes have to be washed or bathed and tucked into their bunks, the older children following later – then peace, perfect peace. Talking of baths, which are usually disliked, especially by boys – these prove very popular because the children have a 'real sailor's' bath in salt water.[2]

Aside from the tremendous adventure of being out at sea, and the wide variety of activities, including imaginary pirate and naval games, children were most impressed by their daily menus, as one young lad noted:

The menu was much to our liking – eggs, bacon, fried tomatoes, pancakes, kippers and oily bloaters with their heads still on. The latter two I ordered daily for breakfast even in the worst of storms and a request that I now understand gave even the cook a turn. There was few of our group there for breakfast on the first day, while not of concern it was hard to fathom. A later visit to the deck above gave reason for their absence. Our fellow passengers were all along the outer deck peering downwards, not so much enjoying the great height as being sea sick on the dock below. Many parents in all their wisdom had assured them they would be ill. Despite the fact that we were still tight to the wharf, they were meeting the family wishes. I decided then I would die before joining them at the rail any time on the voyage.[3]

Letters that flowed home to parents from their offspring on board ships normally arrived in batches, since they were usually lumped together and posted at the various ports en route to the children's destinations. For most parents these letters were the first indication of the routes their children were taking. It was not unusual, for example, for a parent to think that their child was travelling to Canada when in fact they were en route to South Africa or elsewhere. All efforts were made to send sea-vacs to the country of preference stated by their parents, but this was not always possible. Confirmation in this respect only arrived several weeks after the children had embarked. However, regular communication via letters continued to strengthen ties with home, and once children stepped onto foreign shores their host families made letter-writing a priority. Shakespeare had bestowed all host families with guiding principles and the importance of communication was at the forefront of these guidelines. Moreover, although he disliked the nickname of 'Uncle Shakespeare', he nonetheless adopted a paternal role towards his sea-vacs and often referred to British children living overseas as though they were part of his own family, recording in his memoirs that:

> As my family of children overseas grew, parents were naturally anxious to receive frequent reports as to their welfare. A regular correspondence took place between them and their foster parents, and the letters exchanged were full of expressions of gratitude. They were some of the most moving letters I have ever seen. As time went on, correspondents who had never met were calling each other by their Christian names. Through the courtesy of Sir Edward Wilshaw, Chairman of Cable and Wireless, every CORB parent and child could send a free cable each month from the Dominions to their homeland and vice versa. We also arranged with the BBC for the recording of messages from children to their parents and from parents to children. Thus grew the two way talks which became such a popular feature later on in the war.[4]

There were widespread criticisms of the cable and wireless network, however, with some participants claiming that children and adult messages were restricted by censors. Indeed, according to some historians cables were brief and repetitive because participants were required to choose their message from a set menu of brief standard texts such as 'love and greetings from all at home' or 'all well here'.[5] Yet these texts were purely guidelines, and there were thousands of messages that did not adhere to the standard text format. Messages were often quite surprising and, aside from their popularity, radio talks and recorded messages completely dispelled the notion that all children were languishing with homesickness. One young girl who had obviously escaped an unhappy home life in Britain embraced her new environment with enthusiasm, and relished the opportunity to send a cable. Concisely worded, her message reverberated loud and clear, and cut to the quick: 'I thank God that thousands of miles separate me from my stepmother in England!'[6] This was certainly not a message chosen from a set menu of greetings, and others in the same vein confirmed that many children were relieved to have been given the chance to escape home and start afresh in a new land.

Personal messages continued to pass to and fro throughout the war using BBC, Dominion and American broadcast systems, letters, parcels and telegrams. The BBC in particular supported parent and child links with their regular Director of Empire programmes such as *Hello Children*. BBC staff would also chase contacts if necessary, as the following correspondence indicates:

15th April 1943
Dear Mrs McGinty

We were distressed to learn from your letter received today that you have not yet had an opportunity of recording a message to Patricia. It happens that we are holding a session in public at the BBC Exhibition and I am enclosing a formal letter of invitation.

Would you please let me know by return if you can accept, as there will not be another session from Manchester for some time?[7]

The enclosed formal invitation read:

Dear Mr and Mrs McGinty,

We should be glad if you could come to the Art Gallery, Mosely Street, Manchester on the 21st of April at 4 p.m., to record a short message to your child overseas. It will be included in one of the programmes 'Hello Children' to be broadcast in our Overseas Service within the next few weeks. The children concerned will be cabled about time and wave length. If you are able to come the enclosed form must be returned, and completed, to Broadcasting House, London. Your joint message should last for thirty seconds only, i.e. about 90 words.

The BBC is willing to refund travelling expenses in any cases where parents would otherwise not be able to make this journey.[8]

The McGintys duly travelled to Manchester and made their recording to their daughter. Some months later, however, they had still not heard from Patricia. A letter from the BBC, dated 8 November 1943, revealed that there had been problems associated with tracking down their daughter's recording:

Dear Mr McGinty,

Thank you for your letter of October 31st.

It is possible that Patricia has recorded a message which has not yet been broadcast. Unfortunately, owing to circuit conditions we have not received any 'Hello Children' programmes from Australia since May. We have asked the Australian Broadcasting Commission to send us by air mail any programmes which are already complete. When they arrive we hope to broadcast them in the Home Service but, if not, we shall certainly give parents an opportunity of hearing their children's voices.

Should Patricia's message be among those sent you will certainly
be notified.[9]

The level of communications clearly varied between nation states and
exchanges between Australia and Britain often proved problematic. As a
detailed progress report relating to the children pointed out:

> War conditions make it such that the children [British sea-vacs] are not as
> advanced as Australian children of their own age – but they are responding well.
> The children greatly appreciate the fortnightly broadcasts from their parents –
> we still have several difficult cases ... but we have matters well in hand.[10]

The circumstances of war often interfered with and delayed the delivery
of international mail, and prevented some scheduled radio broadcasts. Yet
despite these problems, the BBC did magnificent work in terms of maintaining
links between children and parents. Furthermore, in addition to the personal
messages that plied to and fro across the oceans, official communications also
kept parents informed of their children's educational progress. School reports
were often sent back to Britain and teachers frequently included further sum-
maries that described the home environment of individual children, their
hobbies and pastimes. CORB officials even sent out questionnaires to parents,
which asked whether or not they had any particular educational expectations
for their children or whether they had considered the prospect of their children undertaking technical training overseas.

The responses to these questions indicate that generally CORB parents
wanted their children to have the best education possible. For instance, in the
records of the son of a fitter who was sent to Australia, it was written, 'parents do not wish him to leave school', while the reports of a daughter of a
crane driver, who was hosted in Canada, indicate that the child 'would have
remained at school as long as the work there justified it'. She would have
'taken the HSC and matriculated in order to qualify for a university career.
Parents do not wish her to have commercial or technical training.' Thanks to
the encouragement and financial support of hosts and the Dominion communities generally, many of these parental wishes were fulfilled.[11]

In addition to voicing their preferences for their children's educational
paths and careers, parents back in Britain also committed their own fears and
thoughts to diaries. A father of four daughters who were evacuated on the
same ship to Canada confided in his diary on the day of their departure:

> There are mines strewn across the oceans, submarines lying in wait to
> torpedo them, aircraft searching for them to blow them to pieces. Yet I cannot

but believe that the crime of exposing them at sea is less than the crime of keeping them at home to be the possible victims of an invading army.[12]

Given the fears of most parents left behind, it was no wonder that children were encouraged to write home as frequently as possible. The vast majority of children wrote letters to their parents at least once a week, and the process became an integral part of their routine. It is possible that host families suggested topics for inclusion in such letters, but there is no evidence to suggest that letters were censored. They usually conveyed upbeat messages however, because even young children were aware that their parents needed reassurance. Everyday activities were described along with new and exciting experiences. Children wrote of their inclusion at schools and their daily routines. They also wrote about new friends they had made, and their new hobbies such as dancing, art classes, piano lessons, hiking, mountaineering, skiing, bike riding, parties, skating, bobsleighing, scouting and girl guiding, pony trekking, horse riding and other outdoor pursuits. Positive and cheerful attitudes were expressed in such a way as to uplift parents. The following letter, written by a young girl who had been evacuated with her two younger sisters to Ontario, was typical:

Dear Mum and Dad,

I am very happy in Kingstone. The people are so kind, and I like the school. I am at the Collegiate and I am taking a commercial course. I am changing once again. I am going to the house of the school teacher who took us to Ottawa, she's grand and Edna [younger sister] is going somewhere else, as the lady we are staying with at the present moment cannot afford to keep two children. You see they are getting no money from the government and it's all voluntary. Netta [younger sister] is very happy she is being taught tap dancing lessons and music lessons. I am going to be taught whatever I want too, and Edna is going to take tap dancing lessons. I was working in a big store on Saturday and I made 1 dollar and 75 cents, that is about 8/- and I have that all to myself for pocket money. Not bad eh? But that was because the people were not able to give me spending money. Most likely the house I am going to will not let me work as they will give me money but if I ask they will let me and I would like to, because I could do whatever I wanted with that a week. I did not make any mistakes with the money, it was easy. I love shorthand and typing. The school type writers have no letters on them but that is the best way to learn. I mean when working in the store I just work one day 8 a.m. till 8 p.m., on Saturday only so that's class for getting 8/- to $1-75. I get on fine with arithmetic at school. It's easy! Miss Cummings the school teacher is going to buy me a new winter coat this afternoon. She has already bought me shoes and Mrs Dalgarno bought me a gorgeous hat. She has also bought me and Edna socks, and Miss Cummings I mean, has bought us socks, and me panties and vests and sweater and frock, so I am doing well ...

Give my love to everybody. Netta and Edna send theirs too. Be brave remember we are safe and happy and leading the kind of life you would like us to lead. Remember these are three little Scots lassies praying for their Mummy and Daddy every night and that Good God is watching over them and you.

Cheerio for the present and keep your chin up. There will always be a Britain.

From the eldest of your three daughters
Love from Nancy[13]

By the end of 1940 a good many of the sea-vac children had found part-time work to supplement the income of their families. There were even cases where older children attempted to send money home to their parents. Settled in their new lands, they were nonetheless aware of the misery of rationing, food and fuel shortages, and the money problems caused by spiralling inflation back in Britain. The practice of sending parcels, therefore, was not one-way, and children who had been placed with affluent families consistently sent items of clothing and other gifts across the oceans to their struggling parents.

Communications between sea-vacs and their families also reveal the stoical nature of children. Very few of them complained about their circumstances. Even those who later confessed to having had negative experiences, frequent house moves and extreme feelings of homesickness did not reveal any anxiety within the pages of their correspondence. Instead, radio broadcasts and correspondence between sea-vacs and their parents mainly displayed optimism, common sense and calm restraint. Furthermore, throughout the uncertainty and danger of the war years these same communications revealed the famous 'British stiff upper lip' in action. The communication process became easier in 1943 with the introduction of air-graphs. These were photographs of letters, which were transported as negatives and printed at destinations.

Notes

1   For a more detailed analysis of these children please see: Starns, P., *Blitz Families: The Children Who Stayed Behind* (2011).

2 National Archive Dominion papers, letter written by Miss Fleming, August 1940, also now used as a historical resource for schoolchildren.
3 B. Atkins, Childhood memories of travelling to Canada on the SS *Nerissa*. More details can be found on www.ssnerissa.com.
4 Shakespeare, G., *Let Candles Be Brought in* (1949) p. 266.
5 Fethney, M., *The Absurd and the Brave* (1990) p. 7.
6 Shakespeare, G., *Let Candles Be Brought in* (1949) p. 266.
7 The private papers of Patricia Johnson, quoted in Parsons, M. & Starns, P., *The Evacuation: The True Story* (1999) p. 154.
8 *Ibid.* p. 153.
9 *Ibid.* p. 156.
10 Australian government papers series A2908 ref. A659 1943/1/4132 report into the welfare and progress of British children in Australia, 16 September 1941.
11 Lin, P., 'National Identity and Social Mobility: Class, Empire and the British Government Overseas Evacuation During the Second World War', *Twentieth Century British History*, vol. 7, No. 3 (1996) p. 332
12 Henderson, M., 'Across the Atlantic to Safety', the *Novascotian*, 5 September 2010.
13 Letter written from Nancy Knight to her parents, 1940. Now forms part of the National Archive learning curve for schools.

8

Maintaining National Identity

Measuring levels of perceived national identity amongst the sea-vacs is a difficult undertaking. Indeed, postmodernists would argue that any sense of national identity was an imagined concept, whilst more mainstream scholars have stated that a constructed set of traditions and cultural heritage created a national distinctiveness that gave British subjects some semblance of comradeship and security. Symbolic pageantry, the monarchy, history, pomp and circumstance underpinned a collective British citizenship. In addition to long-held traditions, there was also an undeniable respect for the British Empire that reverberated around the globe. Consequently, wherever they happened to be, British subjects were usually treated with a polite deference within political and social arenas. Popular literature, international youth groups, missionary societies, empire exhibitions, architecture and education all combined to form a standard view of Britain and her empire. Emigration within the empire was seen as reinforcing family connections, and the empire was crucial and integral to the British economy. By the time that sea-vacs set sail there were nearly 400 million people living within Britain and the empire. There were 294 million living in India, 43 million in Africa, 6 million in Asia, 5.25 million in Australasia and 41.5 million within the British Isles. Significantly, colonial acquisitions were separated according to colour and race. Australia, New Zealand, South Africa and Canada were known as the 'White Dominions'. Although all of these states were self-governing to a certain extent, the British government still dictated foreign policy and exerted considerable political influence over domestic and strategic policy. CORB sea-vacs were only sent to these White Dominions and a colour bar was in place to ensure that all children received from Britain were white.

Children who were received in America via the United States Committee for European Children, however, had no such limits imposed upon them. American policy towards sea-vacs was very clear in this instance, and stated that all children were welcome within its borders. Privately arranged schemes in America, however, did exact certain conditions. Children received by Harvard and Yale Universities, for example, were the offspring of notable British academics, and such eugenically motivated schemes were unquestionably underpinned by the sinister notion of creating an intellectually superior British race. Indeed, it is remarkable, considering the events in Europe, that most of these children were housed by prominent academic members of eugenic societies.

Yet regardless of how scholars have viewed and evaluated perplexing issues of national identity, the experiences of sea-vacs suggest that some affiliation to a British ideal was often uppermost in their thoughts. By providing a unique glimpse into the minds of British children who were transplanted onto foreign shores for the duration of war, it is possible to detect exactly what being British meant for thousands of children. They were also given instruction and guidelines in this respect.

In terms of maintaining their national identities, all sea-vacs were given strict instructions as to the character and nature of what it meant to be British. In addition to the four personality attributes discerned by Geoffrey Shakespeare, a sense of justice and decency topped the list, along with sound Christian principles, a sensible, pragmatic approach to life and a polite consideration of the needs of others. British characteristics also included liberal sprinklings of self-sacrifice, courage, and an entrepreneurial and pioneering spirit. Shakespeare's motto and order to 'grin and bear it' when times got tough was epitomised by the legendary stoical British 'stiff upper lip' and identified as a strong and desirable British quality. Children were taught the history and geography of the British Empire, the latter usually denoted by pink areas on a global map. A sense of pride was encouraged and sea-vacs were continually reminded of their ambassadorial role.

'Remember you are British' was the brisk order given to nearly all of the children by their parents and guardians as they hurriedly left the busy docklands of Great Britain bound for foreign shores. Geoffrey Shakespeare was often at the point of departure to repeat this command to CORB children, and great care was taken on board ship to endorse this maxim. Children were instructed to remember their roots with pride. Moreover, in this sense, private evacuees, and those who were evacuated with their schools, were no different to the eclectic mix of CORB children. All were infused with a collective and cohesive sense of shared national pride and heritage. In order to stress this togetherness, sea-vacs were instructed to sing either 'There

Will Always Be an England' or 'Rule, Britannia!' as they approached their destination ports. There was also evidence that Shakespeare's maxim had not fallen on deaf ears:

> Across the other side of Canada, at a small railway station in the early morning, an escort found a small girl of seven weeping bitterly. Suddenly a girl of eleven went up to her and said: 'Stop it at once and be British.'

And the escort recorded that the child immediately pulled herself together.[1]

Yet, once children arrived in their host countries and settled in with their new families, they often struggled to retain their national identity. Furthermore, it was usually the small, everyday events that undermined their efforts to remain attached to their homeland. As a young girl evacuated to Canada, Margaret Hanton was confused by the differing lifestyles between her own and her host family:

> Their standards were different from my own family. I found it distressing that my foster mother would do something that my own mother wouldn't have done. She had her hair permed and she wore lipstick. She wanted me to wear shoes all the time whereas at home I'd been told that shoes scuffed floors and that I should wear slippers around the house. My foster mother wanted me to be 'pretty pretty' but my mother had not approved of me being vain. In the end she gave up trying to prettify me and let me be an intellectual. My foster father was a college lecturer and took pride in the fact that I was clever, and he won the battle. I didn't feel I was in the way. I was very anxious to please. I wasn't secure enough to be bad. My foster mother used to tease me and say 'If you don't behave, I'll send you back to St George Street. That had been the reception centre. I believed her.[2]

In some instances, appearances did seem to matter more than intellect and character, particularly in Canada and the USA. They also mattered to those who were trying to hang on to their roots. There were many examples of children clinging to their British clothes even when they were threadbare, and in Victoria, a group of English schoolgirls insisted on wearing their English school uniforms until they were too small.[3]

Fashion trends in Canada and America were very different to those back home. Young Canadian and American girls wore make-up in their early teens and became interested in boys and romance much earlier than their British counterparts. A few sea-vac girls were assimilated into these trends, but most buried their heads in books, stoutly defended their right not to wear make-up, and steadfastly clung to their own sense of propriety.

In addition to fashion trends and appearances, speech also served to highlight national variations. There was often a substantial age difference associated with the ability to retain British accents. Younger children tended to adopt the accents of their host families, but older children tried much harder to keep their English accent. For instance, a 6-year-old boy from the north of England could not be understood at first by his host parents, but by October 1941 he was speaking 'very distinctly', and possibly his own parents may have had difficulty in communicating with him on his return.

A few children found the English speaking voices of those presenting the BBC World Service odd and somewhat out of touch with ordinary English accents and the varying regional dialects. By the time he was 8, in 1943, one boy's big amusement was to make fun of the BBC announcers.

Older children, in contrast, sometimes struggled to keep their accents out of a sense of loyalty to home. In one family, the older girl tried to keep her English accent and the younger to lose it.[4]

Amusingly, in some households the native children attempted to copy the accents of the guest children. A young Canadian girl, for example, was so jealous of the attention given to a British evacuee living near her in Saskatoon that she locked herself in the bathroom for hours at a time to practise her British accent.[5]

A young English girl named Betty initially became full of self-importance as she recounted the tales of her traumatic ocean crossing, surrounded by attentive and compassionate adults. When such storytelling became boring, she wrote to her father to complain about the unceasing questions and constant attention. Worried that his daughter was becoming a somewhat precocious young lady, he wrote to remind her of her roots: 'You must be very patient and try to like answering questions. Remember that you are a representative of England and you must give people a good impression of English children.'[6]

Undoubtedly the children sent overseas were bound by their ethnic traditions, and those who were sent to families that had been nominated by their own parents fared better and settled down in their new surroundings quicker than those who were sent to unknown host families. Yet when it came to fundamental issues and everyday activities, over 90 per cent of children were confronting the same problems and taking roughly the same period of time to adjust to their new circumstances. Along with English children, the Welsh, Irish and Scottish evacuees were also desperately trying to retain their national identities, and their ambassadorial role was not forgotten. Their appearances and speech set them apart from native children, but there were numerous incidents whereby the latter made every effort to include the guest children. Organisers of youth movements

were also particularly adept at mingling international and native traditions. In America, for instance, campfire gatherings often included both
American and British folk songs:

> Evelyn McNish sang 'The Bonnie Banks of Loch Lomond.' While John
> Anderson, aged 15, taught all the children to sing 'Tipperary' and Peter
> Soundy sang 'Over the Rainbow. They learned 'The Barrel Polka' and 'Old
> Black Joe'. They read American 'funny papers'. The Union Jack flag was
> displayed next to the American flag, and they sang 'God Save the King'
> along with 'The Star-Spangled Banner'.[7]

For the most part guest children embraced their new environments and
experiences with enthusiasm. *Life* magazine reported that 'Evelyn McNish
was learning the jitterbug and several boys were playing baseball'.[8]

In a similar vein the *New York Times* announced:

British Boys Get a Baseball Lesson
Nineteen English refugee boys played baseball at Columbus playground.
Boys aged between eight and fifteen were part of a group of one hundred
children staying at Seaman's Church Institute. Most arrived the previous
Thursday on British liners *Sarmaria* and *Scythia, Carmine, Caruccio*. A
volunteer worker with the Committee for Care of European Children
explained the rules of the game.[9]

In their letters home the sea-vacs often raved about the music, sport and
cultural traditions of their receiving countries. It became abundantly clear
from such correspondence that most sea-vacs had been placed in families
of a higher social class than their own. They were astonished that their
host parents possessed a level of affluence that allowed them to have baths
whenever they wanted, to throw food away in a seemingly wasteful fashion
and to have as many lights on as they liked. One young girl who was evacuated to Johannesburg was spellbound when she found herself surrounded
by servants, sports cars, three-course meals and an amazing wardrobe of
clothes. Others were fascinated by technology. Jean Trevor, the daughter of
a Yorkshire steel worker, was evacuated to relatives in Fort William, Ontario,
and noted that while her mother was still washing by the gas wash boiler,
dolly stick and old-fashioned mangle, Aunt Jenny had an electric washer,
roller irons and an electric cooker.[10]

Yet as P.Y. Lin's study of sea-vacs discovered, such luxuries were not
restricted to the very wealthy. Stanley Buller, the son of a Middlesex garage
mechanic, was hosted by a Western Australian shipping clerk and lived in a

detached, spacious house on its own grounds, made frequent visits to neighbours and spent weekends crewing on the family yacht. Doreen Glance, the daughter of a Darlington steel-mill worker, evacuated to live with a wholesale butcher in Sydney, Australia, was so excited that in her first letter home she wrote: I like Mrs R – because she has a refrigerator and makes ice cream, and I like Mr R – because he has a car and has also a telephone here.[11]

Even small differences in lifestyles were noted by the sea-vacs. Children who were housed in America became accustomed to showers instead of baths or tin tubs in front of the fire. American households did not have egg cups and host parents were bemused when children asked for 'egg and soldiers.' The tube was now the subway and guest children were taught the 'thumbs up' sign. Hot dogs and candy took the place of toad in the hole, and sweets and biscuits were known as cookies. Children who had never travelled further than their local shops and school now found new lives that incorporated a wealth of opportunities, and the sheer size of the receiving countries overwhelmed them. The *New York Times* announced that 'Children praise our New England scenery and find our ice cream greatly to their liking'.[12]

Nevertheless, aside from the razzamatazz and constant attention, the usual problems of homesickness, emotional isolation and feelings of grief and longing for their own families surfaced from time to time. In his memoirs, Geoffrey Shakespeare noted: 'Homesickness is a strange disease; it comes suddenly like a virulent germ, and such is its physical effect on the child that it lowers all power of resistance. But the same child within an hour is laughing and joking again.'[13]

Host parents, guardians, schoolteachers and members of the clergy believed that the trick of combating homesickness was to encourage guest children to be busy all day long. Thus, in addition to their schooling, British children learned to love the outdoors. In Canada they mastered the skills of skiing, ice hockey and ice skating, whereas in Australia they learnt to surf and swim with great gusto. Many of them became accomplished yachtsmen and astute navigators.

Religious affiliations also highlighted national identity, and great care had been taken to match the guest children with families of their own religious denomination. A few children, however, found their host families to be much stricter about religious worship than their own. Presbyterian families, for example, insisted that children said their morning and evening prayers whilst kneeling by their beds, whereas the majority of children argued that they normally said their prayers once they were in bed. Host parents often wrote to parents back in Britain to clarify this issue. Despite the efforts to match children to host families or boarding schools where religious value systems were similar, this was not always possible. In such circumstances, children would frequently take advantage of the situation. A young Protestant English girl found herself in a Catholic Canadian boarding school and attempted to bend the rules to her own satisfaction:

> It was custom for the older girls to attend Mass at six thirty each morning in the school chapel, and this requirement applied to me, even though I was not a Catholic. I really had very little religious conviction of either a Protestant or Catholic nature, but somewhere along the line I had picked up the notion that Roman Catholics were not allowed to attend the services of another denomination. So I stormed into the bathroom one evening before bath time, where I knew sister was on duty, and burst out with an impassioned speech on how wrong it was that I was made to go to Mass in the mornings. 'How do you know?' I demanded, 'that we Protestants are not allowed to go to Catholic services, just as you are not permitted to go to Protestant ones, and here you are forcing me to be disobedient. Of course it was a put up job on my part, but with all the rules, regulations and regimentation of our daily lives I could not take it any longer. Sister withstood this outburst good humouredly but nevertheless reported it to the Headmistress, Sister Maura. The answer came back that, because of fire regulations, the staff could not assume the responsibility of leaving me alone in the dormitory in the mornings in view of the fact that the dormitory was on the top floor of the building, and so, for safety's sake and everyone's peace of mind, I would have to go to Mass. And so I did, with a little white veil attached to my head. That was a battle I did not win.[14]

Children evacuated to Canadian boarding schools struggled more than others to retain their national identity. Host families and voluntary youth organisations were prepared to compromise and frequently made allowances for their small charges, whereas staff working within institutions stuck rigidly to pre-existing rules and individual British children in such establishments had no choice but to comply. But in some cases British schools were evacuated en masse and supplanted in the grounds of stately homes. In these circumstances national identity was shored up on a daily basis by teachers who had travelled to foreign shores alongside their pupils. The largest group to come to Canada with their school were the 160 pupils and staff of St Hilda's, from Whitby in Yorkshire. This school was run by an Anglican order, the sisters of the Holy Paraclete, and the party arrived in Montreal in the summer of 1940. They spent the late summer weeks at Ontario Ladies' College while their sponsors scrambled around trying to gain funds and accommodation for the school. Eventually the head of Trinity College, Mrs Watson Evans, offered the use of her country house, which was set in

90 acres of land at Erindale, near Toronto.[15] Lessons that focused on British history, cultural traditions, empire-building and tales of heroic adventures combined to ensure that no child forgot his or her roots.

There was no doubt, however, that some children were confused about their nationality. A girl named Jean recalled that, 'when we joined the Canadian Junior Red Cross at school, I figured I must be a Canadian because I was invited to join same as everyone else.'[16]

Yet a young boy named David stated,'I always felt at home in Canada; that is I never felt like a foreigner but equally always aware that I was English.'[17]

The same child admitted that listening to English folk music prompted a yearning for his homeland, and he wrote to his parents, 'when I am at school I get homesick! But the only thing that makes me homesick is music.'[18] A deluge of lovingly knitted garments provided by his mother provoked a succinct postscript to his letter: 'I do not want you to send any more sweaters, socks and mitts.'[19]

Religious affiliations, speech, manners, dress codes, music, dance, diet, historical traditions and media attention all combined to ensure that guest children stood out from the crowd. Such children did their very best to adjust to their changing circumstances, and most were pleasantly surprised by their environments. They discovered to their delight that social mobility was a possibility, since social-class barriers were not as rigid as they were in their native land. Moreover, gender discrimination was much less obvious. Two girls evacuated to live with relatives in Durban, South Africa, for instance, noted:

> Although we lived with our father's brother, life was very different. There was no violence, no rationing, kind servants to do tasks we had to fulfil at home. We lived in South Africa in a good residential area in a detached house. As females in this household we experienced no discrimination. At home, as females, we were regarded as unimportant.[20]

There were other signs that the social framework of host countries encouraged gender equality, particularly within the education system. Before the post-war educational reforms, the bulk of children in Britain left school at the age of 14. In Canada and elsewhere, children remained at school until they were 18. Even in regions where poverty was the norm, children still continued their education until graduation. Lynn Codd recalled: 'People's general attitude towards education was that girls as well as boys had equal opportunities and that you were expected to be an achiever to the best of your ability.'[21]

The Australian government adopted the same principles towards education as the Canadian government, and teachers were not averse to chastising parents or guardians in households where such principles were not respected, as Nora Anderson noted:

> The teachers were determined that the narrow outlook of my English born guardians who were of the opinion that girls did not need higher education, as they would just get married, should not prevent me from attaining my potential and went to the trouble of persuading my guardians. In England even if teachers felt that way, they would not have done anything about it.[22]

Thanks to the funding provided by Dominion governments and host families, most evacuees stayed on at school until they were 18 and succeeded in graduating, regardless of their background and gender. In addition to this funding, special educational scholarships were introduced by Dominion education officials to ensure that all intelligent evacuees were sent to university. New Zealand educationalists even gave written assurances in this respect to Geoffrey Shakespeare.[23]

Stephen Hughes, who was evacuated to South Africa, commented favourably on the education he had received:

> When I was finally sent to boarding school in Natal, I very soon settled down, and contrary to my London experience, proceeded to do quite well academically. I certainly stayed at school far longer than I would have in London. I matriculated in eight subjects, with distinctions in four of them, and even managed to reach matric standard in Africaans. This excellent schooling would not have been available to me had I not been evacuated.[24]

Methods of education were also different within the host countries:

> The key to the evacuees' achievements lay in the Dominion's schools' greater emphasis on independence, critical thinking and student opinions; their fostering of education as a collaborative effort between teacher and students; and their broader curriculums which included typing and home economics.[25]

Documentation reveals that as British children became more accustomed to living in their host countries they began to notice the social and educational failings of their native land. Nevertheless, the majority of sea-vacs remained loyal to their country and, despite the obvious and tangible shortcomings of their own country, managed to cling on to some semblance of national identity. They had arrived on foreign shores as apprehensive bundles from Britain, children from the mother country, nervous and shy but full of national pride and identity. After a few years in their host countries, they were confident, healthy and well educated. They had not forgotten that they were representatives of Britain, but simultaneously they appreciated and acknowledged that the experience of being evacuated overseas had given them a broader perspective on life. Their affiliations to their homeland remained intact, but by the end of the war it was supplemented by a wider understanding of other peoples and lifestyles.

Notes

1 Shakespeare, G., *Let Candles Be Brought In* (1949), p. 257.
2 Inglis, R., *The Children's War* (1989) p. 127–9.
3 Bilson, G., *The Guest Children* (1988) p. 126.
4 *Ibid.* p. 109.
5 *Ibid.* p. 107.
6 *Ibid.* p. 76.
7 Manful, H., 'Hoover Evacuees, Part One: A Haven For Children During World War Two' at *http://www.cantonrep.com/x1688624942/Hoover-Evacuees-Part-1-A-haven-for-children-during-WWII/?tag=2*
8 *Life Magazine*, 16 December 1940.
9 *New York Times*, 8 October 1940.
10 Lin, P., 'National Identity and Social Mobility: Class, Empire and the British Government Overseas Evacuation of Children During the Second World War', *Twentieth Century British History*, vol. 7, no. 3 (1996) p. 324.
11. *Ibid.*
12. *New York Times*, 24 July 1940.
13. Shakespeare, G., *Let Candles Be Brought In* (1949).
14. Winter, A., 'Recollections', Imperial War Museum ref. 91/37/1.
15. Bilson, G., *The Guest Children* (1988).
16. *Ibid.* p. 10.
17. *Ibid.* p. 147.
18. *Ibid.*
19. *Ibid.* p. 148.
20. The Patricia Lin Collection, Imperial War Museum, questionnaires 72 & 73.
21. *Ibid.* questionnaire 64.
22. *Ibid.* questionnaire 38.
23. National Archives DO/131/38
24. The Patricia Lin Collection, Imperial War Museum, questionnaire 92.
25. Lin, P., 'National Identity and Social Mobility: Class, Empire and the British Government Overseas Evacuation of Children During the Second World War', *Twentieth Century British History* vol. 7, no. 3 (1996) p. 329.

9

Sea-Vacs in Canada

In terms of numbers, Canada received the largest batch of British children evacuated via the CORB scheme, and also the largest number of privately evacuated children. A total of 1,502 children were sent through CORB, and over 10,000 through corporate schemes and private arrangements. A further 5,000 travelled through Canada to reach destinations in America. When the call went out for suitable host parents to volunteer their services, much of the overwhelming response was due to pre-existing and long standing imperial relationships. The communication networks between the British and Canadian business arena gathered momentum, as did those between academic institutions. Consequently, professional people such as doctors, politicians, lecturers and lawyers began to offer homes for the sea-vacs. There were also incidents in which whole schools were relocated away from British soil and incorporated into a number of Canadian private schools. These moves were initiated by Major F. J. Ney, executive vice-president of the National Council of Education in Canada, who firmly believed that youth migration schemes were vital for the post-war reconstruction and futures success of the empire. This was not a view shared by all. The nation's prime minister, Mackenzie King, for instance, regarded juvenile migration as needless and potentially politically destabilising. The immigration department, under the directorship of Mr F.C. Blair, also adopted a cautious stance with regard to British sea-vacs, although by June 1940 the department conceded that European children could enter as refugees and, in view of the immediate emergency threatening Britain, Canada would waive temporarily certain restrictions imposed by immigrant status for British children and their mothers. The latter, therefore, were viewed as evacuees rather than refugees. This definition of status was important because evacuees dictated the level of inclusion within their host families. Children billeted in medical families frequently accompanied doctors on their house calls, while those who were billeted with dignitaries and officials often went into their offices to observe and assist them with their paperwork. In this manner children became accustomed to the adult world and accepted in the wider community. Across the length and breadth of Canada, sea-vacs were encouraged to stay on at school and to aim high. Children recalled with pleasure the dynamic teachers who taught them with enthusiasm and energy. Most were young and newly qualified, but they inspired children with a broad curriculum and a relaxed teaching style. British children were amazed to discover that their new teachers were far more approachable and less inclined towards disciplinarian regimes. Even CORB director Miss Maxse, who had so vehemently criticised welfare schemes, was very impressed by the standard of education offered to sea-vacs. Some CORB children who had left their schools in Britain at the age of 14 found that they were expected to go back to school in Canada in order to achieve a standard matriculation level. Miss Maxse reported that 'in some cases the provision [for education] was even better than that available for local Dominion children, as when generous foster parents or a local reception committee paid the fees for evacuees to attend independent schools, including boarding schools'.[16]

By 1942 the majority of British children had settled well at school and were looking forward to planning their career paths. In the same year, however, parents of children evacuated to Canada began to demand their repatriation. It had become obvious to most people by this stage, both at home and abroad, that Britain was unlikely to be invaded. America had joined the war in December 1941 following the attack on Pearl Harbor and British parents were convinced that the war would not last for much longer. Anxious to be reunited with their children they bombarded the CORB office requesting that officials organise immediate and safe passage home for their offspring. CORB also received similar requests from those parents who had sent their children to Canada by private means. A few of these had been accompanied by their mothers. This latter group had been struggling for some time with the British ban on sending sterling to a country using the dollar. In addition, there were other groups of sea-vacs who had come of age during the war and, eager to dispel the notion that they were avoiding the bombs and war service by being abroad, they pleaded for passage home in order to join the armed forces. In Canada, 80 per cent of eligible CORB boys joined the forces – around 40 per cent joined the Canadian military and the remaining 40 per cent were enlisted into the British military. Girls were also keen to help with the war effort and over half of the CORB girls joined the Women's Auxiliary Services.[17]

In response to an increasing number of requests for repatriation, CORB organised the return of sea-vacs via the 'White Ensign Scheme'. This scheme permitted commanding officers in the British Royal Navy to take on board certain previously selected civilians and take them back to British shores. These civilians were usually fit young men who wanted to return home to join the armed forces. Thus a mid-war flow of returning evacuees began, firstly as a trickle and later as a flood. CORB increased the level of repatriation from Canada in 1943 by providing passages for CORB boys aged 16 and over and girls aged 17 and over. This provision was, in theory, available to CORB children living in all Dominions, but the war in the Far East precluded most such ventures. Parents who had children living in other Dominions, therefore, were simply not made aware of the scheme. There were instances where children did manage to return to Britain from other Dominions before the war had ended – some even became stowaways – but they were not assisted by CORB.

According to a summary of CORB's work, written by Miss Maxse in 1944, Canada was afforded special praise for its educational endeavours, although statistical information suggested that at least 10 per cent of sea-vacs failed to adjust to their first homes and were subsequently rehoused. Where these same children failed to settle in their second homes, whether because of personality problems, abuse or severe homesickness, Miss Maxse wrote sympathetically, suggesting that the wisest and kindest course of action would be to send these children home to their parents.[18]

Statistics do not, however, reveal the full extent of misery suffered by a minority of evacuees. There were many who later reported some form of abuse and criticised the fact that CORB representatives only ever interviewed them at home and usually in front of the host parents. If representatives had interviewed evacuees at schools they may have gained more insight into their individual circumstances. Those children who were experiencing difficulties more often than not adopted a 'stiff upper lip' attitude and simply put up with their situation for the duration. When they were later given the opportunity to confide their troubles to their parents, offenders were usually brought to justice. Undoubtedly these abused children suffered severe emotional distress and tried to erase their memories of Canada. But for the majority of children, those who were lucky enough to be placed with loving, caring families, Canada was a wondrous country. Their overriding memories were of outdoor hikes that lasted for weeks, camping expeditions, and holidays in the Rockies. In addition, as they learned to play ice hockey and developed the skills of skiing, skating and sailing, friendships were formed that lasted a lifetime. Moreover, the gratitude of British parents was overwhelming. The mother of Douglas Penwarden, for instance, paid tribute to the Canadian people as follows: 'Douglas received the great advantage of being able to get away from the war terrors of Britain, and being treated royally by every person whom he came into contact with in Canada.'[19]

Letters expressing similar sentiments continued to flow into CORB headquarters throughout the war. Those who lived as sea-vacs in Canada later claimed that their experiences had encouraged a sense of independence, freedom, self-assurance and forbearance. Their experiences also prompted a tidal wave of emigration from Britain to Canada in the immediate post-war period.

Notes

1 National Archive DO131/29.
2 Mann, J., *Out of Harm's Way* (2005).
3 Fethney, M., *The Absurd and the Brave* (1990) Appendix VII p. 302.
4 National Archive DO131/28 & DO131/33.
5 Bilsom, G., *Guest Children* (1988) pp. 116–18.
6 Fethney, M., *The Absurd and the Brave* (1990) p. 157.
7 *Ibid.*
8 Bilsom, G., *Guest Children* (1988) p. 147.
9 Fethney, M., *The Absurd and the Brave* (1990) p. 195.
10 *Ibid.* p. 193.
11 *Ibid.* p. 171.
12 *Ibid.* p. 164.
13 Bilsom, G., *Guest Children* (1988).
14 Lucy Tipton was the daughter of a Middlesbrough steel-mill plater. The Patricia Lin Collection, Imperial War Museum, questionnaire 47.
15 Vera Longworth, The Patricia Lin Collection, Imperial War Museum, questionnaire 98.
16 Miss Maxse, 1944, 'Summary of the work of CORB', National Archive D.O.131/35/43.
17 National Archive DO/131/27.
18 Miss Maxse, 1944, 'Summary of the work of CORB', National Archive D.O.131/35/43.
19 Fethney, M., *The Absurd and the Brave* (1990) p. 194.

10

Australian Sea-Vacs

When compared to the governments of the other Dominions, the Australian government was very quick, with regard to sea-vacs, in resolving guardianship issues. National Security Regulations 1939–40 for overseas children appointed the Minister for the Interior as guardian for all overseas children, a position that he delegated to child-welfare authorities in all Australian states with the exception of Western Australia and Tasmania, where delegation was to Overseas Children's Reception Committees.' Custodians of sea-vacs were given strict guidelines and were expected to provide them with good accommodation, suitable nourishment and clothing, appropriate schooling, time to enjoy leisure pursuits and healthy exercise. They were also expected to provide moral and spiritual guidance, and to treat the children as members of the family. In addition, official guidelines stated that household chores performed by children needed to be suitable for their age and physical development. Representatives of local authorities were responsible for ensuring the adherence to these guidelines and for overseeing the general welfare of 577 CORB children and over 10,000 privately evacuated children. Most of the latter group were placed with previously nominated relatives, and by 1940 over 5,000 letters had poured into government offices offering to provide homes for non-nominated incoming children. The CORB liaison officer in Australia, Mr W. J. Garnett, had already made certain recommendations with regard to the welfare and billeting of children, and whenever possible these were followed to the letter.

According to Mr Garnett, all homes needed to be inspected before the children arrived. He suggested that where possible siblings should be placed in the same home. If this was not an option then siblings should at least be placed in the same community. Billeting officers were also advised to take heed of friendship circles and to endeavour to keep them in the same neighbourhood. The social class and religious affiliations of children needed to be recognised in order to place children in families that had a similar background to their own, and institutional care, except for problem children, should be avoided at all costs. CORB officials were advised to keep a low profile and only offer guidance to local authorities when it was necessary.

In a similar style to Canadian host parents, the motivations of Australian hosts were mainly altruistic. A Mrs Goyen, who adopted a 6-year-old boy from Edinburgh, did so because she wanted to repay a kindness: 'My father had been wounded during the landing at Gallipoli. He convalesced in Manchester where he received much kindness. We decided to take an evacuee to help repay the kindness.'[2] Australian relatives of British children also felt that they were doing their bit for the war by housing nieces, nephews, cousins and sometimes even younger siblings.

Upon arrival in Australian ports, sea-vacs stayed in residential accommodation for a few nights while they awaited their hosts. Non-nominated children usually had to wait longer to be placed, and nearly all children were required to make further long journeys by train to their final destinations. Significantly, individual states and the Australian government footed the bill for evacuee care. Moreover, although British parents were paying 5*s* a week towards the care of their children, Australian hosts maintained that they did not want to be paid. Their contribution to the war effort was wholehearted and required no funding whatsoever. As Senator Foll, Minister for the Interior, stated, it was desired that true Australian hospitality should be extended to these little guests from the old country.[3]

As with the Canadian experience, children who had further still to go after arriving in port were well cared for on their journeys across Australia, as a report compiled by Mr Honeysett, who acted as one of the escorts, revealed: 'The staff on the train from Sydney to Brisbane gave unstinted devotion to the welfare of the children ... the children were entertained at stations along the way, Coffs Harbour, Casino and Kyogle. The reception given to the children by the people of Queensland was magnificent.'[4]

For the young sea-vacs, Australia was a vast outdoor playground. They became accustomed to an open-air lifestyle with immense beaches and a varied countryside. They generally lived in large, airy houses that were set back from the roads in beautifully landscaped gardens, with a variety of household appliances such as refrigerators and vacuum cleaners that were new to the children. There were verandas and fly screens, sun lounges and outdoor furniture; an abundance of wildlife, such as koalas, snakes, deadly spiders such as the funnel-webs and redbacks, and kangaroos and sheep; and they soon adapted to a sunny climate that favoured outdoor living.

The majority of CORB children were billeted with city families or with families who lived in the suburbs. Around one-fifth of children, however, were housed in the seemingly limitless bush, often with relatives. Muriel Evans from Yorkshire went to live with her aunt in Bullsbrook, Western Australia, and at first glance believed that her aunt lived in a cowshed. She described the homestead as follows:

> It was a weatherboard house with an iron roof, and a veranda all grown over with honeysuckle. There was a pepper tree and a mulberry tree, a hen run, and further away there was a paddock where the cows wandered. Beyond that was the real bush. The house had no taps. We got water out of the brook with buckets, and used rain water from the tank for drinking and bathing the baby. In the summer we used to put the water in kerosene containers, and stand them in the sun to get the water hot enough to have a tin bath. Later my aunt bought a concrete bath and we perched it in the shed. It only had a plug hole, no taps or drain.[5]

Aside from the obvious hardships, living in the bush could be lethal. Barbara Donald recalled that her schoolhouse was built on stilts to deter dangerous spiders and snakes. Barbara always took precautions and carried a razor blade and some magnesium potash to rub into a snake bite before spitting the poison out, and she was warned by her teacher not to try and kill the snakes. Muriel Evans recalled the safety instructions: 'If you saw a rat you were supposed to run away; if you saw a snake you had to stand still and shout "SNAKE!" – and hope somebody would come. You had to look for another snake because they went around in pairs.'[6]

Although bushland was wonderful for long hikes, bike rides to primitive shacks and picnics, children could easily get lost in the vast expanse of a terrain without landmarks. Bush fires caused by heatwaves were also a problem; families would pack up all their belongings whenever a bush fire started, just in case the fire became uncontrollable.

For sea-vacs based in cities and towns, social life often revolved around youth groups initiated by a variety of churches. Football and cricket tournaments were organised for both girls and boys, and singing and music lessons were offered to children of all ages. Scout groups and girl guides also provided a focus for outings and other leisure pursuits. Welfare programmes were well organised and children were subjected to frequent medical inspections. The director of the Child Welfare Department received quarterly medical reports, and these included a list of transfers and changes of addresses pertaining to overseas children.[7] In terms of child placements, children were usually billeted with parents from a higher social class than their own.

This process was to some extent unavoidable, because the bulk of volunteer hosts came from the higher social strata. Furthermore, although the Australian government were prepared to pay 10s a week for overseas children, they fervently hoped that most children would be billeted within families who were happy to raise the children unaided. But welfare officials, although efficient at maintaining a child's physical well-being, often ignored the problems that were associated with placing children in families of a different religious denomination. Moreover, a few hosts proved to be obsessively pious. John Hillier, for instance, who rarely went to church back home, found himself attending three services with his host every Sunday, while John Fethney was irritated by his Methodist hosts:

> The first Sunday we were there he made the assumption that we'd all go off to their Methodist Church together. I more or less insisted on going to the local Church of England. I think they thought it was a bit pedantic but I'd been confirmed before I left home and I was already thinking of the ministry.[8]

Religious and socio-economic considerations aside, welfare workers did their best to maintain strong links with the overseas children and monitored their progress at regular intervals. However, many of the children who were initially billeted with friends and relations needed to be rehoused. A memorandum written on 16 September 1940 concluded: 'Out of a total of 479 children, 317 have been virtually consigned to relatives and friends who have not voluntarily offered to take them.'[9]

These reluctant hosts were not ideal and usually contacted the relevant welfare departments to demand that children be relocated. Around 18 per cent of CORB evacuees resided in three or more different billets. Yet there were other sea-vacs who felt overprotected by relatives, many of whom firmly believed that they needed to shape British children's development in such a way that Australian culture did not impact upon their characters. Joyce Briant, for example, felt suffocated by her aunt and uncle:

> We got to a state where I felt that I couldn't put up with it anymore. In the end I said 'Oh well, I think I'd better go. I went into my room and started packing my case, but Auntie came in and started unpacking it. Uncle said, 'If she wants to go let her go.' We had a bit of a barney but it cleared the air. I got what was worrying me off my chest, and they then knew that if anything was worrying me we could sort it out. We got on fine after that. Everything was English orientated. Auntie was English, and she didn't want me to pick up any slang or talk Australian. She wanted me to go back the same little girl that I'd come out. But after Pearl Harbor it looked as

though the war was going on forever. 'You're not going back to England just yet, not for a year or two,' I thought. 'It's silly to think that everything back home is best! I then started really enjoying Australia and I got to like it very much.[10]

Some children were billeted in very luxurious surroundings and there were amusing incidents as they adjusted to their new-found wealth. John Fethney, then aged 13, son of a Bradford municipal clerk, was occasionally given a lift to school by his first Australian host, Senator H.S. Foll, Minister for the Interior, travelling in the Senator's chauffeur-driven, government-registered Buick. One day John arrived at North Sydney High School late for class. In response to a master's tetchy objection, he said – with a suitably deadpan face – 'Sorry Sir! The chauffeur was late today.'[11]

The Fethney brothers were eventually moved to Woolagong, where their billet, owned by a doctor, backed onto glorious beaches and countryside:

The back garden sloped down to a creek. There was a bridge over it into a paddock, and beyond that was another paddock, both of which Dr Palmer owned. Then you began to climb up the mountain, up the Illawarra escarpment, straight into the bush. On our hikes we'd usually penetrate a bit beyond the top of the escarpment, then have a picnic, grill some chops over an open fire – all this was part of the thrill of Australia. I sometimes imagined, facing west over the escarpment with the bush stretching away, walking for hundreds and hundreds of miles. Apart from crossing a few tracks you could just walk on and on and eventually reach the Indian Ocean.[12]

Yet this beautiful environment was no substitute for a loving family unit:

In all sorts of ways we were very much a part of the family, but I think there was a formality that was something of a barrier. For instance, no-one ever suggested more intimate forms of address than 'doctor' or missus. Our Yorkshire taciturnity probably didn't help, but neither did the doctor's very quiet and rather nervous manner. His wife was very moody and I used to think that perhaps I'd offended her.

However, there was nothing strong enough to run away from, or dare to say to the occasional social worker 'No we're not alright,' I think the thought of having to start again somewhere else was even worse than putting up with her ongoing moodiness. If one could have escaped ... if there had been an offer, one would have to consider very carefully. Do we start off with yet another family where it wouldn't be perfect? Or do we go on putting up with the known – on balance, yes we do.[13]

For the Fethney brothers, compliance was probably the easiest option, and there were many others who put up with adverse situations. Compared to some Canadian states, Australian child welfare officers were far more efficient. However, there was a tendency to overlook evacuees who were placed with relatives; there was an assumption that these children would automatically receive a high standard of care, yet this was not always the case. An 11-year-old girl who was billeted on her uncle's farm was subjected to sexual abuse:

> Every night when I went to bed I used to pray that something would turn up so that I could get away from the whole situation. I didn't know what I would do if something didn't turn up. When the Japanese came into the war my aunt said that it would be much safer for us all to be sent inland. So my sister, two brothers and I were sent to two families in Wagga, for which I was eternally grateful. It was terrible to live through. It made you feel, especially as you were told that you mustn't tell anybody, that it was partly your fault. There was no-one to confide in. I often wished that there had been somebody from CORB, but I never saw anybody. It stayed with me for years after I came home. I told my mother after the war, but I loved my father very dearly and I just didn't want him to know that his brother had done such things.[14]

Undoubtedly child welfare officers did their best to prevent and detect forms of child abuse, but a recurring theme amongst the sea-vacs was the notion that remaining in unsatisfactory homes was preferable to moving elsewhere. A child's fear effectively deterred them from making complaints, since conditions in a new home might actually prove to be worse than their existing residence. There was also evidence that children who moved frequently became more emotionally disturbed than those who stayed put. Some children simply remained restless. A 14-year-old boy from Yorkshire, for example, failed to settle with any foster parents. He joined the Australian armed forces but was found to be under the recruitment age limit. As soon as he reached 18 he returned to England, assisted by CORB officials, and joined the British Army.[15]

Child welfare departments did, however, offer a degree of protection from exploitation. Even in 1944 when an Australian Army liaison officer suggested that CORB girls could be released to undertake clerical work with the Army in India and Ceylon, welfare agencies stepped in to prevent such recruitment strategies. But although child welfare was reasonably effective, Australia did not match up to Canada on the educational front. Whereas the Canadian education system required all children to stay on at school until they were 16 years of age, and then encouraged children to pursue further education, it was impossible to detect the same ethos within the Australian education system. Children in Australia, as in Britain, could leave school at the age of 14. Furthermore they were not, as a matter of course, encouraged to continue in further education. Girls in particular had a rough deal, since it was assumed that they did not need an education because their primary function was to get married and bear children. Consequently a large number of girls did not reach their full potential. A young Welsh girl living in New South Wales, for instance, was forced to leave school to take up clerical work even though she was a high academic achiever and desperately wanted to become a doctor.[16]

The official government view was somewhat mixed with regard to university places. The policy, such as it was, merely stated that custodians of overseas children should not be expected to provide university training for children in their care. The Australian Universities Commission suggested that only a few overseas children desired to further their studies at university level, and it was assumed that suitable children would receive scholarships.[17] Thus, higher education in Australia was reserved for the minority of sea-vacs. Therefore, although CORB children in other Dominions attained considerable academic achievements; a significant minority, especially amongst those in Australia, felt they had made limited progress compared with what they expected to achieve.[18]

Despite the lack of funding for university places the guest children still appreciated the way in which subjects were taught in the schoolrooms, and the openness of the school grounds. British schools were generally grim, gloomy Victorian buildings with limited concrete playgrounds. By comparison, Australian schools were modern, airy constructions set in huge grounds with well-maintained football and cricket pitches, tennis courts and vast landscaped play areas. Classrooms were built with large windows that let in the sunlight. Children were encouraged to enter debates about their subject matter, and to learn through projects. This was a distinct departure from the 'chalk and talk' teaching methods that still held sway in mainstream British schools. There was also a greater emphasis on sport.

The degree to which sea-vacs settled in schools largely depended on the other pupils around them. Native children either smothered sea-vacs with attention, regarding them as a novelty, or they teased them mercilessly for their accents and their lack of knowledge with regard to Australian culture. Teachers tried to incorporate British history, language and poetry within a broad-based curriculum. As time went on, however, sea-vacs began to forget their time in Britain and for some this process was alarming and distressing. When they were given the task of describing a variety of British plants in spring for example, most simply could not remember what these plants looked like. Other children found themselves on an emotional rollercoaster as poetry struck a heartfelt chord and prompted sudden bouts of homesickness. Michael Fethney was told to study Rupert Brooke's poem 'The Soldier' along with the rest of his class, but he resisted learning it for homework because of the words 'If I should die ... there is some corner of a foreign field': 'I didn't want to die at the age of twelve. I know that wasn't what the poem was about, but the teacher insisted that I learn it. We ended up with her in tears and me in tears during the lunch hour.'[19]

For the majority of children, however, Australia was an opportunity to enjoy new schools, the wonderful beaches and wide open spaces. Marjorie Ursell, who was billeted on a dairy farm in Victoria with the brother of her father's work colleague, recalled her time 'down under' with fondness:

> I cycled four miles to school each day along long country roads. The two daughters of the family did the same, and we all went to technical school. There I was someone special and everyone had just that bit of sympathy and really looked after me. It was so healthy to spend my early teens in such fresh air, such exercise, such fun trying to ride that horse. The Saturday ride along the road a couple of miles to collect the daily mail and deliver it to the neighbours on the return; more often than not I was kicked off Malonga's back, he just hated this chore.
>
> It was a new and happy time for me, the family were very caring and the life style was outdoors ... suddenly I was 'someone' and fussed over and spoilt at school. The last year in Australia I spent at the domestic science college living in a girls club run by the Methodist Church organisation in Melbourne. The daughters in the family also attended the college. The boys went to war and sadly Alan the eldest son never came back from Singapore.[20]

The fall of Singapore in February 1942 sent shockwaves through Australia and, at a time when Canadian sea-vacs were thinking of returning to Britain, Australian sea-vacs were beginning to fear for their safety, since the war was suddenly on their doorstep. On 19 February Darwin was bombed by the Japanese, and Australians became anxious about the possibility of an invasion. CORB officials in London sent reassuring messages to parents, and children who were deemed to be in vulnerable areas on the coast were relocated further inland. Parents were kept informed of any change of residence. Members of the Australian government were severely disappointed that Britain and her Allies were throwing all their efforts into winning the war in Europe whilst leaving Australian forces without any back-up defence.[21] Several piers were destroyed by the Australian government because it was thought that Japanese soldiers might use the piers to assist an invasion. Mines were laid on beaches and other possible landing points.

Male sea-vacs who were coming of age in terms of being eligible for military service were encouraged to enlist in the British Army in India. After a period of six weeks in the army the recruits were able to apply for commissions. They attended a routine selection board meeting and many young British lads became army officers by this route. CORB girls of recruitment age tended to enlist in the Women's Auxiliary Services. Younger children also did their bit for the war effort, making essential supplies for the military. Scout groups were particularly involved in this process. Their mind-numbingly boring tasks were conducted primarily on the coast of New South Wales, where they made camouflage netting for the air force by putting fragments of hessian into the netting. Children were allowed time off school, usually in blocks of three to four weeks, in order to complete this crucial war work.

As the war in the Far East continued, British children in Australia became despondent, especially once the war in Europe was over. In May 1945, scenes of the Victory in Europe celebrations dominated the cinema screens and most guest children had naively thought that they could return home as soon as European hostilities had ceased. Instead, they were caught up in another conflict, the result of Japanese ambitions of territorial expansion.

The Japanese surrender was only assured following the devastating effects of nuclear attacks on Hiroshima and Nagasaki in August 1945. The bulk of children had little knowledge of the atom bombs and their consequences, but they did understand the meaning of the Japanese surrender, as Marjorie Ursell recalled:

> I had been taking part in college competitions and had a great time with all my friends on V.E. day and then at last it was V.J. day and preparations to return home. This time it was a journey of only six weeks, up through the Suez Canal and the Mediterranean Sea. Home and such a welcome, it had been a long time. Such problems though because we were not the little children who went away.[22]

By this time, however, it had become clear that many British children wanted to remain in Australia. Thus CORB officials were busy advising the parents of these children of the application procedures for emigration, in addition to organising passages home for children who did want to return to their homeland. The high number of parents who took the opportunity to emigrate at this time is testimony to the level of hospitality their children had received.

The mother of Derric and Catherine Webster, who were evacuated from Bradford to Melbourne, stated: 'The Australian hospitality was amazing, and they made many friends. They enjoyed school. They became confident and self-reliant.'[23] Evacuee Freda Stout echoed this view: 'I adored my years in Australia. I shall never forget the kindness and hospitality of the people. It was incredible.'[24]

In response to numerous enquiries, CORB established an emigration programme under the Children and Parent Settlement Scheme, whereby the British government would pay for the parents' passage and provide them with financial assistance to help them settle. The Australian government also actively supported this emigration process and provided financial assistance to all of those children who were seeking to remain in their country, and to their parents.[25]

Notes

1 Fethney, M., *The Absurd and the Brave* (1990) Appendix VII p. 302.
2 *Ibid.* p. 157.
3 Australian National Archive A659/1940 /1/7570. Senator Foll, speaking on 16 January 1941.
4 Australian National Archive A659/1940/1/7621.
5 Stokes, E., *Innocents Abroad* (1994) pp. 141–2.
6 *Ibid.* p. 144.
7 Australian National Archive A659/1944/1/355.
8 Stokes, E., *Innocents Abroad* (1994) p. 136.
9 Australian National Archive A659/940/1/7577.
10 Stokes, E., *Innocents Abroad* (1994) p. 127.
11 Fethney, M., *The Absurd and the Brave* (1990) p. 175.
12 Stokes, E., *Innocents Abroad* (1994) p. 139.
13 *Ibid.* p. 128.
14 *Ibid.* pp. 165–6.
15 National Archive DO/131/29.
16 National Archive DO/131/94.
17 Australian National Archive A659/1943/1/4703.
18 Fethney, M., *The Absurd and the Brave* (1990) p. 216.
19 Stokes, E., *Innocents Abroad* (1994) p. 134.
20 Ursell, M. B., memoirs and diary held at the Imperial War Museum ref. 96/55/1.
21 For a complete analysis of the political relationship between Great Britain and Australia during the war please see Gay, D., *The Great Betrayal*.
22 Ursell, M. B., memoirs and diary held at the Imperial War Museum ref. 96/55/1.
23 Fethney, M., *The Absurd and the Brave* (1990) p. 194.
24 *Ibid.* p. 191.
25 National Archive DO/131/35.

11

Kiwi Brits

The majority of children who arrived in New Zealand had been at sea for about forty-eight days, and when they reached their destination they were tired, hungry and apprehensive. A few of them had contracted scarlet fever, measles, impetigo, heat rashes and boils en route. These children were quarantined in council buildings and hospitals, whilst the others continued on their journeys. A progressive and tolerant New Zealand government approached the care of overseas children in an entirely different way to the other Dominions. It was the only administration to organise child welfare from the pinnacle of central government, and to have welfare issues inextricably linked to existing educational systems. The Children's Emergency Regulations were introduced in 1940 and placed all evacuees under the care of the Superintendent of Child Welfare, who was also an officer of the National Department of Education.[1] Thus, responsibility for the placement and follow-up care for CORB children rested with officials from the welfare division of the national government's education departments.

In terms of numbers the country only received 202 children via the CORB scheme but over 1,000 private evacuees had also found their way to the Dominion. In addition, whole cohorts of Scottish children were sent to Wellington.

From the outset New Zealand welfare officials had decided that children arriving in the country would be escorted to their destinations by the very people who had escorted them over the oceans. Escorts aboard the RMS *Rangitata* and *Ruanhine*, therefore, were expected to stay with the children until they reached their placements rather than leaving them at the port of arrival. Newly arriving children, therefore, did not experience the uncomfortable limbo of waiting in unfamiliar surroundings with strangers until placements were found. Placements were usually organised well in advance of a child's arrival, but in some instances officials were still rushing around at the last minute to find suitable billets. A chaplain aboard the RMS *Rangitata* recorded:

> I took a party of fifty children to Auckland. We were accompanied by several local officials. About thirty of the children were going to relatives in various parts of the island. Most of the children were collected in Auckland, but I took several to places further north. The remaining twenty were allocated to homes in Auckland. There were a thousand applications for them, so the local committee had some difficulty in deciding to whom they should go. Great care was taken to place children in homes with a congenial environment, for example the son of a policeman was, if possible, placed in a policeman's home, and so on. I saw some of the homes, and have returned to England quite convinced that the children are well and happily placed.[2]

Volunteer hosts and their homes had been vetted, and the Mayor of Wellington arranged meetings with youth and church leaders to establish welcoming committees for the CORB children. In addition, the same guidelines that had been laid down for the well-being of children by Mr Garnett in Australia were followed by the central government administration in New Zealand. Furthermore, because New Zealand was a small country in comparison to the other Dominions, it can be argued that it was easier for welfare officers to implement these recommendations. Indeed, the latter made every effort to promote a close relationship between hosts and welfare departments, as the following letter dated 26 August 1940, which was sent out to prospective hosts from the Wellington City Young Britons Committee, clearly demonstrates:

> Dear Sir/Madam
>
> I have to acknowledge with many thanks the receipt of your application for two of the children to be evacuated from Great Britain. His Worship the Mayor has set up a committee which has undertaken the responsibility of placing the children in suitable homes and environments. With this end in view a contact committee has been set up to interview applicants in their own homes, to establish a friendly contact between foster parents and the committee and obtain what additional information is required. Would you therefore, kindly receive two members of the contact committee to interview you in your own home at your convenience? The two members detailed to visit you will ring you to make an appointment and will carry

with them a letter of introduction. I trust that these arrangements will meet with your approval ... [3]

Visits to prospective hosts were extremely thorough and took into account the age of hosts, the presence of existing children, socio-economic backgrounds and religious leanings. Of all the Dominions' officials, those in New Zealand displayed the highest levels of professional competence when it came to dealing with children. The centralised welfare provision undoubtedly contributed to this excellent standard of care. Throughout the war, however, eighty-two CORB children were rehoused on at least one occasion and twenty-three were rehoused on three or more occasions. Moreover there were two fatalities: a young science student died whilst rock climbing during his holidays, and a young girl lost her life following a series of operations to cure her facial cancer.[4] Furthermore, although New Zealand statistics reveal a higher standard of child welfare than elsewhere, they do not necessarily expose levels of unhappiness. Nevertheless it does appear from personal statements that the vast majority of CORB children were contented in their new homes.

A young lad recalled his departure with his sister from Bristol, and his arrival in Auckland:

I was not aware at the time that we had been chosen from 'deprived families'. I was not sad to leave. Home was a tiny terraced house with a small back yard and the remains of our neighbour's house across the road staring at us through our cracked front windows. I shared a bed with the lodger and felt hard done by most of the time. We lived near a crossroads and every night the anti-aircraft gun arrived and disturbed us more than the Germans ever could as mum, my sister and I tried to sleep under the stairs. Dad and the lodger curled up under the table during prolonged raids. At school we spent a great deal of time in the damp, smelly shelters under the school playground and our education was beginning to be seriously disrupted on a daily basis. I was however, up to date with the 'Sea-Vacs' serial in my weekly comic so I knew exactly what to expect. There would be fun and games and I would be the hero who sighted the u-boat periscope and saved the convoy!

Eventually we arrived at Wellington and my sister and I were in a party who were sent off to Auckland. We travelled overnight by train, passing real volcanoes and arrived at our destination early next morning.

It seemed that no-one wanted a pair so Joyce and I were split up. I went to a very rich family in Remuera and Joyce to a working class family on the other side of the city. We met once a fortnight for a couple of hours to play. I was overwhelmed by my new family. They had a large house in what seemed to be a park to me. They had two cars and their back garden had its own lagoon where all the boys had their own small boats, sailing dinghies, canoes etc. They had a large property to the north of the city with its own private beach where we spent holidays. I knew I was not in Bristol, finding myself in an environment where boys did not play out in the street and where strange things like doing dishes, cleaning your own room and helping cut the lawns were part of everyday life. I had hard lessons to learn. My foster mother was sweet and kind and looked after me. My foster father was quite strict and supervised me having cold showers every morning and scrutinised every piece of work I had to do.[5]

The majority of sea-vacs in New Zealand were nicknamed the Kiwi Brits, and were spoilt and feted. It was not unusual for host families to find gifts of sweets, cakes, toys and other treats left on their doorsteps for the guest children. Clearly people felt sympathetic to their plight because they were so very far away from home. Once again, the evacuees were usually billeted in upper-class homes. Three sons from Glasgow, for example, were taken in by the manager of General Motors. As the evacuees approached his enormous mansion house, his servants lined the entrance as a mark of respect to the arriving evacuees. The youngest son remembered his experiences within the home with fondness: 'We had no problems whatsoever. We were not separated. Our foster home was superb. We fitted into school life very easily. I feel certain we had no emotional or physical difficulties, or anything else that bothered us or our foster parents.'[6]

A boy who lived in several homes was more circumspect with his hosts:

After nearly two years there was some sort of illness in the family and I had to move on. I found myself with an elderly couple in the middle class area of Parnell. It was pleasant enough and I was allowed to have outside friends. My new foster mother felt that I was too young to clean myself at the age of twelve! She spent an awful lot of time giving me a daily bath. At least I had no daily chores to do.

This situation only lasted a few months. They had a son in the R.N.Z.A.F. and he was invalided out after an accident. There was no room for me to continue staying so I was on the move again. There was some difficulty finding me another home this time. The novelty of poor English children had obviously worn off. A place was eventually found for me with relatives of the family my sister stayed with. My new foster parents were an eighty-six-year-old Maori princess and her unmarried daughter who had recently had a stroke. Here again I became a bit of a drudge doing gardening, grass cutting and generally finding life hard. No chores, no pocket money.

Nevertheless I was not far from my sister. After a while I settled down and began to enjoy myself. I made many friends, including my first girl friend. I had a short period at grammar school and won a scholarship to the school of art.

I joined the boy scouts, where I managed to become acting troop leader before returning home. I took up a paper round which gave me pocket money and a certain amount of independence. As I learned to work hard I earned the respect of 'Grandma' as I used to call her, and she was a fund of interesting Maori history and customs. I learnt much from her.[7]

In total, only twenty-three children were moved on three or more occasions. Welfare workers carried out inspections in the homes of host families every three months and their monitoring procedures were rigorous. Problems were usually identified quickly and resolved with astonishing efficiency. As time went on, however, there were fewer volunteers available. In part this later reluctance to take evacuees was due to the change in the course of the war. In the beginning both hosts and sea-vacs believed that the war would not be a lengthy affair. Indeed, many ex-evacuees were adamant in their claims that their parents would not have let them go to foreign lands if they had thought for one minute that they would need to remain there for five years. Initially, therefore, as the children began to settle down and appreciate the beauty of New Zealand, especially wildlife and the Rotorua mountain range, hosts assumed that their small charges would only be with them for a maximum of two years. But as the war dragged on and the Japanese conquered a large number of key strategic areas in the Far East, New Zealanders, along with their Australian neighbours, began to fear an imminent invasion. They also began to acknowledge that British children might be with them for far longer than they had originally expected. Thus, volunteer hosts were thinner on the ground from 1942 onwards.

In spite of this ongoing problem, in the latter years of the war child welfare programmes in New Zealand remained cohesive, competent and centrally controlled. Every effort was made to monitor children in their respective schools and to supervise their progress in the field of health. The New Zealand government also provided the best and most plentiful educational opportunities for evacuee children, second only to South Africa. The school-leaving age in New Zealand was identical to that in Britain, but secondary education was free for all in New Zealand and children were encouraged to study long past the age of 14. British children were found to be better at English and history than the native children, but slightly behind on subjects such as mathematics and science. The majority caught up quickly, however, and ascended to the top of the class, where they usually stayed.

Furthermore, those who had struggled in British classrooms found a new lease of life in the Dominion's schools.[8] In preparation for a speech to the British Victorian League, Geoffrey Shakespeare highlighted the fact that all Dominions had established a scholarship system to assist bright children, but New Zealand in particular, had made every effort to enable intelligent evacuees to attend university.[9]

According to the 1944 report summary compiled by CORB welfare officer Miss Maxse, around 8 per cent of evacuees had been accepted for university degree courses, technical training, teacher training and higher educational courses. This figure included sea-vacs in all Dominions, but children were far more likely to stay within the education system in New Zealand and South Africa than elsewhere. Over 90 per cent of children remained in education until the graduation age of 18. Across the board, however, girls lost out on educational courses. Intelligence tests revealed that over 80 per cent of girls were capable of reaching high academic standards, yet over two-thirds of these girls were channelled into doing menial tasks or pressed into clerical work.[10] Male high achievers, however, usually had their pick of degree or training courses. For those who were less academic, farming was a great attraction for many young boys. The New Zealand government introduced a youth farm settlement scheme. Along with five years' training and financial incentives, the scheme offered assistance to young men eager to establish their own farms. Some Australian states offered similar schemes.

But it was not merely the variety of educational opportunities in New Zealand that encouraged large numbers of older children to remain in higher education. The majority did so because they were unable to enter the armed forces at the age of 18: the call-up age for military service in New Zealand was 21, therefore, there were fewer CORB boys recruited into the armed forces there than there were in other countries. Around 30 per cent of CORB boys, however, on reaching the age of 18, decided to reject education. Instead, they found passages back to Britain in order to join the British forces. Some even became stowaways to achieve this aim.

CORB officials were responsible for the return of evacuees but, as with Australian sea-vacs, those residing in New Zealand were adversely affected by the war in the Pacific. An official CORB letter to parents outlined the position:

When hostilities in Europe are over, the CORB children will be able to return immediately shipping is available, and I hope that there will not be much delay. I am afraid, however, that it will take longer to arrange passages of children in South Africa owing to the greater distance and to transport difficulties, while the return of children in Australia and New Zealand will depend on the conditions in the Pacific and Indian Oceans.

> To all parents I would say that there is no reason to worry, the Board will do its best to see that the children are brought home as soon as safe passages are assured and as soon as there are ships to carry them.[11]

There was also a growing recognition that many children wished to stay in New Zealand and the other Dominions. These were children who were studiously attending university courses or busy carving out career pathways, or in some cases they were simply children who had escaped unhappy backgrounds in Britain and were reluctant to return. CORB responded positively to those who had successfully adjusted to the Dominions:

> The Board has been asking parents not to bring their children back without their written consent, as in some cases their children have found good openings in the Dominions and wish to stay there or the parents themselves wish to go out and join their families. I can assure parents who fall into this category that they will be consulted in writing before any arrangements are made for their children to return. The Board has always foreseen the possibility that some of the children evacuated under these auspices would wish to take advantage of the opportunities open to them in the Dominions and that neither they, nor their parents, would wish them to return to the uncertain conditions which will, at any rate for a certain time, prevail in post-war Europe.[12]

Certainly a large number of older children remained in New Zealand and some who initially returned to Britain later emigrated to the Dominion. A male sea-vac described the repercussions of leaving his host country once conflict had ceased:

> My little world came to an end ... I was not allowed to continue with my art studies and found it hard to settle down. After a year or so I ran off and joined the Royal Marines where I found a home for over twenty three years. My parents and I tried hard to understand each other but we remained virtual strangers until they both died. Sadly, I could never appreciate how they felt and whilst the great adventure may have made a different, better person of me it did nothing towards the deep personal relationship that should have existed between me and my close kin. Even so, in retrospect, I would not have missed the experience. My sister Joyce, very wisely, returned to New Zealand many years ago where she still lives happily.[13]

Reflecting on his reluctant departure from New Zealand, 16-year-old Colin Crafer recalled happy memories of his three different foster homes:

[My] continuing desire to own a pianola like the one in my Mount Pleasant home; the school at little river and my friendly contact with Maori children; learning the facts of life – that a dozen chickens can pick a cooked sheep's head clean in fifteen minutes; and finally, as a worker in Christchurch fitting and turning, collecting wages, my first bicycle – and leaving it all to come 'home.' I often wonder why.[14]

The delights of living in New Zealand were recorded in detail within the pages of children's diaries, along with experiences that surprised them, events that made them laugh and occasions of celebration. Many of the diary entries focused on the type and quality of food they were able to eat. Evacuees were totally amazed, for instance, that New Zealanders sometimes ate steak and eggs for breakfast, or pancakes and waffles with maple syrup and fresh fruit. The children also enjoyed eating the wide variety of fruits that were new to them, such as the kiwi, papaya and passion fruits. After the restrictions imposed by rationing back home, children gained weight quickly and thrived in an atmosphere where food was varied and plentiful. In addition to savouring new foods, the children also explored the magnificently dramatic open countryside. They were particularly in awe of the volcanoes and hot geysers, and many of their diaries and letters home contained pictures of the same. Diaries also record a surprising atmosphere of melancholy when hostilities ceased and the time came to board their homeward-bound ships. Most of sea-vacs had been happy in New Zealand for five years and could not remember home. Subsequently over 70 per cent of them returned to New Zealand as soon as the opportunity arose.

Notes

1 Fethney, M., *The Absurd and the Brave* (1990) Appendix VII p. 302.
2 Report compiled by the Chaplain of the RMS *Rangitata* September 1940
3 *Ibid* p.158.
4 National Archive DO/131/43.
5 Porter, J., further memoirs can be found at the War Time Memories Project.
6 Fethney, M., *The Absurd and the Brave* (1990) p. 191.
7 Porter, J., memoirs.
8 National Archive Official CORB history DO/131/43.
9 National Archive DO/131/43.
10 National Archive D.O./131/28, Information given by Geoffrey Shakespeare to the Victorian League July 1941.
11 The private papers of Patricia Johnston quoted in M. Parsons & P. Starns, *Evacuation: The True Story* (1999) p. 160.
12 *Ibid.*
13 Porter, J., memoirs.
14 Fethney, M., *The Absurd and the Brave* (1990) p. 234.

South Africa

T he South African government deliberated for some time before decid-
ing guardianship rules for children arriving from overseas. Local reception committees were established for new arrivals and the Minister of
Social Welfare was appointed guardian under the 1940 Control and Care of
Overseas Children Regulations, but these regulations were not fully opera-
tional until January 1941. In total, 353 CORB children were sent to South
Africa, but over 5,000 private evacuees were also received by the Dominion.
A National Advisory Committee of the Overseas Children's Administration
insisted that local magistrates should have jurisdiction over local reception
committees.[1] Volunteer hosts were vetted in the usual way and, as with other
Dominion countries, a mixture of altruism and patriotism underpinned their
offers of hospitality. A daughter of a South African host noted, 'My father was
asked by his brother to have the girls for the war. My father felt deep family ties
with his brother, Thomas, and, being of British stock, felt very patriotic.'[2]

Ironically, given the fact that South Africa had flatly refused to receive
Jewish children under the CORB scheme, the majority of British children
were housed in the Cape Town Jewish orphanage on arrival and kept for an
indefinite time to await collection. The remainder were housed in official
buildings such as Westbrooke, the Governor General's home in Rondesbosch,
Cape Town. Some children were collected directly from these buildings whilst
others awaited escorts to take them eastwards and northwards by train. This
latter group were often left in limbo for three or four weeks. A young boy
recorded his happy times in the Jewish orphanage in his diary:

> When we arrived we were given some food and allotted to our dormitories
> and we went to bed at eight thirty. Next morning Saturday 21st September

I woke at seven thirty. I washed and explored around us. Behind our home there is the famous Table Mountain. This morning it had its 'cloth on', which means that the clouds are covering the top of the mountain. The home is very, very modern. We talked to the Jews for some time. Most of the morning we went for walks up the side of Tafen Berg (Table Mountain). We had a nice dinner and in the afternoon we went back to Lady Buwodas house to a big party. There we were welcomed by the Mayoress of Cape Town. Then we were welcomed to South Africa by a South African boy and girl. After we had had some bottles of lemonade and some buns we were driven home by a lady in a car. In the evening I talked to 'Monty' a boy scout, who lives near the orphanage, and goes there for prayers. He was a very nice boy. I went to bed at ten o' clock.

Next morning, Sunday, I went to church. There we were welcomed by the Bishop of Madagascar. We walked back through some gardens after the church service. It was very hot so we were glad when we got into some buses to take us home. After dinner we were taken to Muizenberg by car in the afternoon ... it is a famous seaside resort in South Africa. We had tea there, and when we arrived back at the orphanage we had pictures, and some of the films were very good. I enjoyed it very much, and I went to bed about ten fifteen after a very enjoyable day.[3]

Most days were organised so that children were kept busy. This was a strategy employed to stem homesickness, and a way of introducing as many people to the sea-vacs as possible. Bio-scopes, or the 'pictures' as they were called, were shown to the children every other day. Hikes, sport, parties and official gatherings dominated their lives while they were in the orphanage. After a while, however, as children were collected and the numbers diminished, the ones who were left behind began to feel restless. Furthermore, when there were large numbers of children in the orphanage, activities were structured to keep a child's attention all day long; but as numbers dwindled, so did the activities. Later entries in the same lad's diary reveal his concern:

The lady in charge of us took us to a Woolworth stores where she bought me a bottle of hair oil, some sweets and other things. After that we were taken home by car. In the afternoon I went for a walk, my friend 'Monty' was the guide. After the walk we had some P.T. training. Nothing much happened in the evening, so I went to bed about nine thirty. Next morning, Tuesday, I went to Plata-Clip, which means flat rock. I enjoyed the morning very much. In the afternoon we waited for the eclipse. I watched the eclipse which was very interesting. In the evening there was a party. I went to bed about nine o' clock.

Next morning Wednesday 2nd October I woke up at seven o' clock and had a shower. Nothing happened in the morning, afternoon and evening. I went to bed at nine o' clock. After breakfast next day we went to sea point where we had a swim, which was very cold. I weighed myself today and found that I have put on three pounds in the last two days this makes it thirteen pounds since I left England. After dinner, some children left for their new billets. Then again after supper some more children went off to their new billets. Some were going to Johannesburg, Port Elizabeth and Benoney. Now there are about twenty nine children left in the orphanage. All of my friends have gone and it is not very nice being by myself.[4]

The children who stayed at the Jewish Cape Town orphanage varied in age and gender. A young lad who stayed for some weeks in the orphanage ended up living in five different homes and his time as a sea-vac was more eventful than most:

I went first to a holding centre at the Cape Jewish orphanage where I stayed for about six weeks. I then went with a batch of children and an escort by train to Johannesburg. I do not recollect clearly how we were chosen, but I was selected and went with a couple who had obviously been vetted by the reception committee which was led by a lovely lady called Mrs Meyer. The house where I stayed was very nice and it was on the edge of town. I was treated well and started to go to a local school. I do remember very clearly going for a walk in the countryside and finding a bullet, which I think must have been a 303. I took this back 'home' and went into the couple's shed, where I put the bullet in the vice and with a hammer and nail I detonated it. There was an almighty bang. I was completely disorientated, I could neither hear or see for quite some length of time, eventually my senses returned, I found that the window of the shed had blown out, the head of the bullet had gone right through the toe of my shoe and apparently passed between my big toe and the next, only slightly burning me, the case had flown out of the vice and struck me under the right eye, which was already swelling and completely shut. Nobody had heard the bang, so I went to my bedroom and got in bed. About two hours later the lady of the house called me for dinner, when I said I was not hungry she guessed something was wrong, as a ten-year-old growing lad was always hungry. When she came into my bedroom and pulled back the eiderdown she screamed and rushed off to call her husband; after getting the doctor and ascertaining that there was no life threatening damage I was truly in the dog house. Mrs Meyer was summoned and I was moved to another house within a few days. This only lasted a few weeks and again I was shifted. Altogether I was in four houses before Mrs Meyer herself took charge of me.

I loved her home, her husband Mr Theo Meyer and their son Nigel were all very nice to me; I remember the study had book shelves lined with National Geographic magazines, which I read for hours. However, due to their social and work schedules I was put into boarding school. Firstly I went into St Georges Home for Children, then to Jeppe High School and finally to Houghton College. It was whilst I was at St Georges that I was in a scout group and we were camping somewhere up north of Pretoria, each tent held three boys, and when it was about 3 a.m. the back of the tent was ripped open and a male lion's head appeared in the gap. I was the nearest and my screams immediately woke the other two lads and we fled under the opposite side of the tent. The screams were obviously sufficient to scare the lion and wake up the rest of the camp, but in the meantime the three of us had rushed up the nearest tree. By this time everybody was wide awake and wondering what had occurred; we gabbled on about the lion, but it was only when the tracker studied the ground behind the tent that they believed us. It was a very big lion, to which I could not have agreed more.[5]

Another 10-year-old boy stayed for a mere two weeks at the institution and remembered the day he was collected to be placed in a host family for five years:

We were eventually put on a train to Durban, which went via Johannesburg, a three day trip. One stop was at Kimberley where people gathered to see us. They gave us a basket of large bars of chocolate, which looked good but were actually full of weevils and they soon went out of the carriage window. Most of the children got off at Johannesburg, but about twenty of us continued on to Durban. There we were lined up on the station platform with our labels prominently displayed, while our prospective hosts walked up and down making their selections. We were extremely fortunate to be chosen by a Mrs Stainbank, a wonderful lady who lived at Coedmore, a large estate outside Durban.

The main house was built in 1885 by Mrs Stainbank's late husband, the original pioneer, who came from England as a young man. It was in the style of a large English country house. Two sons and their families lived in bungalows on the estate, which was run mainly as a dairy farm. A large part of the estate was natural African bush, which contained a variety of wildlife, several species of antelope, monkeys, bush babies, snakes, iguanas and birds of every size and colour.

We were brought up as part of the family and were always treated as such. Mrs Stainbank was a lady of almost Victorian values, which she instilled in her family. England was always referred to as 'home.' She had lost one son in France in World War One; another son returned safely. Sadly, she died in 1942. Her eldest son took over as head of the family and we transferred to one of the bungalows to live with Mrs Stainbank's spinster daughter, Edith, who became our 'mum' in every way. We had a very good local education and as the years passed we came to love Coedmore and life in South Africa.[6]

The vast majority of children evacuated to South Africa had pleasant experiences and healthy environments child welfare officers attempted to monitored children across a wide geographical area and compiled reports every six months. There were however, a significant minority who displayed emotional symptoms such as enuresis, rashes, nervous ticks and frequent headaches. Furthermore, despite the efforts of welfare workers a few children escaped their attention for long periods and suffered as a result. The vastness of the country, transport difficulties in isolated terrain, and a shortage of trained child welfare officers resulted in some children falling through the net. A boy who experienced serious neglect described his unusual hosts:

> The five years of my evacuation left scars on my soul. I was billeted at first with a middle-aged, eccentric English couple who hated everything South African. As a ten year old I was terrified of them and hated them as only a child can, especially as I took to the South African way of life like a duck to water. My official guardian was a kindly Scots lady. She did all in her power to have me shifted; but this was overruled politically. However, she had me sent to a farm for the holidays.[7]

In this instance, the farmer and his wife became 'grandfer and grandma' to the boy every holiday. Then, after he had started secondary school, having by now spent three years living with the anti-South African couple in term time, the school matron discovered he was suffering from 'Natal sores,' a disease caused by malnutrition that was unheard of in an European child.[8] There was a storm of protest. As the boy explained, 'I became a 'train boy,' and commuted from grandfer's to school each day. Life became wonderful. I had the joys of a farm life, with riding, shooting and working with ox teams, and love.'[9]

A 14-year-old girl evacuated with her 12-year-old sister and 6-year-old brother also had reservations about her billet: 'The host mother was a demanding, strong personality. He was quiet, retiring and very kind, but not interesting in rearing another family. I don't think any of us can say we were happy. We each had educational problems too, and battled until we finished school.'[10]

The 6-year-old boy had bed-wetting problems and was made to wash his sheets as a punishment. Yet the girl still claimed that 'we were wonderfully cared for, and had everything we could ask for. The South African authorities just could not do enough for us.'[11]

Complaints from children varied in scale from those who simply felt unloved to those who were experiencing severe neglect or abuse. A few children grumbled that they were always introduced to their hosts' friends as their 'war effort.' One girl complained that her hosts were too aloof and explained her emotions: 'I was well cared for but not loved. I felt that I was someone for them to show off, 'their war effort.' I was always introduced as our war evacuee! How I longed for someone to kiss me for myself and not say "for your mother".'[12]

As with the other Dominions, South Africa followed the trend of placing overseas children in homes that were far more affluent than their own. Barbara Clark, for instance, was the daughter of an Essex headmaster. She was used to a moderate middle-class lifestyle back in Brentwood, but on her arrival in Johannesburg she was billeted in the home of an army officer. The large mansion-style house contained servants, and the luxurious surroundings included a double garage, a tennis court and landscaped gardens. Wealth and status ensured that she became accustomed to three-course meals at least three times a day and baths on alternate days. In addition she also acquired a huge wardrobe of clothes.[13]

Muriel Folger also discovered a whole new world, as she was plunged into an intellectual family. Muriel was the daughter of a London clerk who lived with her cousin who was a professor and manager of the theatre at Cape Town University. Within this environment she acquired a broad knowledge about literature, philosophy and educational frameworks. The conversations between academics enriched her education and gave her the confidence to pursue a career.[14]

Despite the gaps in the child welfare system the majority of sea-vacs lived in happy homes and became well-adjusted children. Those who failed to thrive, and those who were suffering from some form of neglect or abuse were referred to as ill adjusted children, and this terminology was recorded on their health records. The placing of children within families was, to some extent a lottery, especially amongst those who were not nominated to stay with relatives. One man recognised his own good fortune stating:

Looking back on my war time African experiences I realise how lucky I had been with the family and home that by chance I had been evacuated to. So many similar overseas evacuees had a very tough time and do not want to remember. But we found kindness and warmth with everyone, especially in the schools we attended where we were called 'war guests.'[15]

It can be argued that welfare initiatives were not always effective, but in stark contrast the educational opportunities that were open to CORB children and other evacuees were excellent and would not have been available to the children back in Britain. The school leaving age was 16 and the curriculum varied and conducive to learning. Wealthy host families often sent their evacuees to elitist boarding schools, and a few were sent to such private schools by anonymous benefactors. Educational opportunities were life changing in nature and the lack of discrimination between girls and boys fostered a community of high achievers. The daughter of a railway clerk for example went first to college and then to university and became a music teacher. Back in Britain the same girl would have left school at the age of 14 and been channelled into office or shop work. Furthermore, the range and scope of educational pathways led to more children studying at university level in this Dominion than in any other. This trend was reflected in the army recruitment statistics. Whereas 80 per cent of Canadian CORB boys joined the armed forces on reaching recruitment age, only 72 per cent of South African CORB boys signed up for military service when they were eligible to do so; because all children were encouraged to stay in higher education until their graduation.

Yet whilst evacuees were mainly enthusiastic about the excellent educational and training opportunities on offer, they were less enamoured with other aspects of South African life. Racism was rife, widespread, clearly visible and completely at odds with British ideas of tolerance and liberalism. South African politicians were turning their back on British political ideology and embracing notions of white supremacy and racial segregation. The policy of apartheid did not become entrenched until after the war, but the seeds of apartheid were already ensconced within all sections of society throughout the years of conflict. This situation was particularly difficult for the evacuees to come to terms with; and several could recall awkward incidences where they were chastised for trying to help black South Africans with their everyday tasks. Indeed most of them felt extremely uncomfortable with this state of affairs and asked probing and pertinent questions of their host parents and of church leaders – questions that could not easily be answered. Therefore, although the majority of sea-vacs enjoyed their stay in this Dominion, they had severe reservations about the way black South Africans were treated.

Notes

1   *The Times*, 22 January 1941.
2   Fethney, M., *The Absurd and the Brave* (1990) p. 157.
3   Diary of G.W. Medway, Imperial War Museum ref 12/23/3.

4   *Ibid.*
5   Wartime Memories Project.
6   Memoirs of Roy Unwins, documented for the BBC. www.bbc.ww2peopleswar.
7   Fethney, M., *The Absurd and the Brave* (1990) pp. 212–13
8   *Ibid.*
9   *Ibid.*
10 *Ibid.* p. 203–4
11 *Ibid.*
12 *Ibid.* p. 205
13 Lin, P., the Patricia Lin Collection, Imperial War Museum, questionnaire no. 52.
14 *Ibid.* Questionnaire no. 2
15 Memoirs of Roy Unwins, documented for the BBC. www.bbc.ww2peopleswar.

13

Homecomings

The repatriation of British children was, in many respects, an ad hoc affair. The government had pleaded with parents to leave evacuated children with their host families until the war was over. This plea applied to all parents of children involved in domestic and overseas evacuation, but parents eager to be reunited with their children did not pay much attention to this official advice. A 'Stay Put' propaganda campaign was implemented, which asked parents to be sensible and toe the government line on this matter. This campaign also fell on deaf ears. British children in Canada had started to trickle home from 1942 onwards, although unbeknown to the parents, dangers still lay ahead in the form of the German V1 and V2 rocket attacks. Many of these children, however, were older and they returned home primarily to join the British armed forces, though a significant minority also wanted to be back with their biological parents once the threat of a German invasion was no longer on the cards. A sizeable number of children were also repatriated from America, and by 1944 the offspring of Oxford and Cambridge academics, who were evacuated courtesy of Yale University evacuation schemes, were flowing back to Britain in large numbers. Logistically, the process of early repatriation of children was a nightmare that depended on available shipping, and often the goodwill of the captain and crew. For children who were evacuated to South Africa, New Zealand and Australia, early repatriation was simply not an option. Only evacuees who were of recruitment age managed to reach British shores from these Dominions, and most of these did so with the help of CORB. Official government planning for a general repatriation of children did not begin until February 1944. The majority of children, therefore, were repatriated after hostilities ceased. However, some children were aboard homeward bound ships as news of the Japanese surrender came through. The *Ruahine*, for instance, left Auckland just before Victory in Japan Day. When the news broke out aboard ship there was much celebrating. From this point on children could be found on almost all ships bound for Britain from the Dominions and America. Official CORB figures reveal that by February 1946, at the last meeting of the Advisory Council, most children who had been evacuated under the British government's official scheme had either returned to Britain or were about to do so:

Canada 1,326 out of 1,535
Australia 446 out of 577
South Africa 284 out of 355
New Zealand 153 out of 204[1]

Yet the long-awaited prospect of homeward travel was not necessarily greeted with whoops of delight by the sea-vacs. Most of the younger children had been little more than toddlers when they arrived overseas and could not remember their parents or home surroundings. Tearful farewells were therefore common across the Dominions, as children left their adoptive homes in order to return to their real homes. The strength of emotional ties to biological parents varied enormously, and host parents were often bereft and distraught at the loss of their wards. Where communication networks between biological parents and their children had been maintained, the latter were more accepting of the homeward journey. But in instances where communications with the homeland had fallen by the wayside, children had responded by forging new and strong emotional ties with their host families and friends. Indeed, the moving and poignant dockside scenes that were prompted by the searing wrench of children leaving their host parents were almost unbearable to watch. There were those whose little faces were so red and wet with tears that they were no longer able to speak the word goodbye. Some children did not even wave in the right direction because their eyes were blurred by the stream of tears. Host families had given the children small keepsakes and souvenirs, or books and poetry. Some of the sea-vacs' friends were even inspired to write their own poetry. The following is an extract of a poem written by an American schoolgirl named Cotton Mayer to her homeward-bound friend:

Dearest Bridgy

For your amusement aboard the boat
While you cross the lengthy moat

And think back to your days at Dobbs
Geometry and howling mobs
Of friendly girls who miss you so
But very glad that you could go
Remember us oh Bridgy dear
With a smile not a tear
And when the Dover cliffs you spy
And in England's fairest sword you lie
Remember Dobbs in early spring
With violets, outdoor mock and the bling
Of tennis balls against the nets
Recall the haze of late sunsets
The early may-day morning dew
Laura and Jane who quite scared you
With their rough play and American manners
Remember when you see the banners
Of England's red white and blue
That three thousand miles from you
A group of people remember well
The day you left and the weary bell
Which called them away to study hall
And hardly let them say goodbye at all
But just think back over the brighter days
The senior dance and the faculty play
Those late Sunday mornings you could laze
And dream or study all through the day
Some days the snow dulled down our life
Sometimes elections eclipsed our time
And now you see I have trouble with rhyme
And no rhyme with life – all I can find is fife
Which makes little sense as my poetry too
So I must apologize deeply before you
As an idiot before a learned scholar
Whose learning is not worth a dollar
But now Bridgy dear as you sit and gaze
And think back on the nicest days
I wish you luck to carry you far
Across the days that ahead may mar America for you
We're truly quite nice though a bit too few
With our manners our voices such things you see
But I hope you'll remember us at the very best we can be.

Lots of love
Lots of luck just me Cotton

P.S. Keep her safe and keep her well
Keep her happy over the ocean swell.[2]

Poems and keepsakes aside, for the most part British children had very mixed feelings about returning home. Moreover they innocently and naively believed that they could go back and visit their host parents whenever the mood took them. They had no concept of the logistics and distances involved with sea voyages, nor of the money needed to secure ocean-going passages. It should also be noted that some evacuees did not return to Britain until 1947 because of the lack of available shipping.

Foster parents Mr and Mrs Goddard, who gave a home to Bob Bullard in Western Australia, remembered clearly the events that surrounded his departure:

He wanted to take everything with him, including a push bike, which required, together with everything else, a box six feet by five feet. When he left he said 'I'll just have a look at everything in England and come straight back,' but it took thirty years before we had that pleasure.[3]

There was no final official assessment of the lives of British children who were privately evacuated overseas, but the final government report, written by the diligent Miss Maxse, concluded that 9 per cent of CORB evacuees stayed overseas. However, this report did not include the youngsters who had joined the military and were subsequently demobbed overseas. By February 1946 just over half of the CORB children sent overseas had returned to Britain. Reliable figures for the thousands of privately evacuated children are not available. Nevertheless, it is clear that a large number of them did not want to return to Britain, and queues for visas to enable mothers to join their children in America for instance, were nearly a mile long. The immigration department at the American Embassy opened an extra annex in order to deal with the overwhelming number of applications. Canada House was similarly swamped with applications from prospective emigrants, along with the remaining Dominions. Consequently a number of CORB officials were designated the task of advising British parents with regard to the rules of emigration.

For the children who did return to Britain, family reunions and subsequent experiences did not always live up to expectations. Britain in 1946 was battle scarred, with bombed-out buildings and rubble littering nearly every city street. People were war weary with anxiety lines etched into their faces. They were poorly-clothed and thinly built. Rationing was still in place and fuel shortages had left many feeling the bitter frost of one of the coldest winters on record. The following extracts taken from the memoirs of sea-vacs sum up the homecoming experiences of many:

> We went by train to Waterloo where our parents met us. I had difficulty recognising them as the war had aged them beyond their years.
>
> I was struck by the grim faces and drab clothes of the people and the general greyness of the buildings, accentuated by the fact that we had left South Africa in midsummer, full of colour and sunshine. How we missed that sunshine![4]

> My Aunt in Australia had a very soft-spoken Australian accent and my Mother had a high-pitched Yorkshire accent and that was the first thing that hit me when I returned home, I didn't recognise her voice.[5]

> There was bread, jam and margarine on the table. I helped myself and everybody stared at me and told me that it had to last a week because we were rationed. You could have either jam or margarine, but not both. We had lived the life of Reilly. I'd had too much food in Canada![6]

> I did not recognise my mother. She had dark hair when I left, and she was almost white when I got back. She'd lost a son at sea, she had two sons in Australia, and she'd had to cope with my younger brother growing up when my father was away for long periods.[7]

> We disembarked onto a small island that was approaching winter. Everything seemed grey, everything seemed small. There was no colour. It was dingy, dismal, austere, and awful. Everything was cold, dark and drab. The people looked tired and worn, the cities dirty, war damaged, and very different from Australia. The train journey from Liverpool to Bradford was increasingly depressing. It wasn't so much the bomb damage but the fact that it was getting misty and murky – just four o'clock and it was getting dark.[8]

> As we pulled into the platform I saw mum, her two sisters and my gran. They all ran along the platform, I leapt out – I'll never forget it – to see them all again. My dad was standing quietly at the back, waiting for all the women to get their tears over with. Dad had hired a taxi, which was a big thing then, and we cried the whole way home. It was so cold, but it

was lovely to be home. Mum and I shared the same bed that night. I kept getting up to get things out of my case to show her, and we talked until the day broke. I couldn't believe the beautiful green – it was all green and all mine. There was a band on the dock, and I cried and cried. The next morning there was ice crackling on the ground. It was lovely![9]

For a young lad named Keith, it was the journey home that was most memorable:

The life aboard a troop ship was wonderful, with all the happiness of war being over, and all going home. No black out, no danger and amateur shows. We were welcomed by Fleet Air Arm planes in the Clyde. This troop ship was named *Ile de France* and we docked in Greenock only five days after leaving Halifax.[10]

Yale Alumni recorded that:

The Oxford and Cambridge parents have sent many appreciative letters to the host parents and the Yale Committee. For some children repatriation was a slow process. One mother wrote to a host – 'At the moment he talks about home referring to this house and yours equally, he calls us both mother impartially and sometimes calls me by your name. So that it seems as if he is finding it possible to slide from one background to another without being conscious of any violent change. The one thing he admits to missing is the comics, and he loves to talk about America to anyone who will listen.

Another parent stated: 'The happy way the returnees are settling down, even if there is a short period of querulousness, greatly removes parental anxiety. They miss everything in America, their friends, schools, and their sports, but they realise that they have come back to their own, where they belong.'[11]

Once the majority of sea-vacs began to settle down in their own homes and communities, they were increasingly shocked at the state of their bombed-out homeland. Furthermore, they encountered a good deal of public resentment because they had experienced an 'easy war.' They were often harassed, teased, bullied and nicknamed 'Bomb Dodgers'. Career pathways that sea-vacs had planned in their host countries were also immediately undermined as soon as they set foot on British soil.

Barbara Wood, the daughter of a York railway signalman, was told by her tutor that he was 'not going to let her teach with that dreadful Canadian accent'. When looking for employment, 18-year-old Arthur Jay was informed that his Canadian school graduation certificate was considered valueless, being from a colony, and not up to the English Grammar School standard and that vacancies were only kept 'for young people from English schools and the returning armed forces'. Other evacuees were immediately rechanneled from academic tracks to technical and commercial schools due to inadequate French or Latin. Joan Myles, the 16-year-old daughter of a mill worker evacuated to Canada did not return to school upon her return to Britain due to the 'incompatibility' of her schooling, despite her intention to go on to university had she remained in Canada. Edward Stoye, the son of a Middlesbrough painter and decorator who was hosted by an engineer's family in Canada, was subjected to such hostility regarding education that with his family he immigrated to his host country. He stated:

> I went back to England before entering High School. I arrived just in time to write the eleven plus exam. Needless to say I didn't do very well and was relegated to a Secondary Modern School. Such a placing excluded me from attending university or even a technical college – of course my parents appealed but got nowhere. I remember being given an intelligence test by the principle of the school. He heckled me as I did the test and naturally I didn't do it well. I think my parents' experience with the English education system was the reason we all moved to Canada in 1947. Here I did go to university. [12]

In fact the secondary modern system of education did not preclude the possibility of admission to university or technical college, but it did make the process more difficult. Due to the circumstances of war the British education system had virtually collapsed by 1940 and had not fully recovered, despite the educational reforms introduced by the 1944 Butler Education Act. But whereas the state system was not renowned for its innovative teaching methods, a few private schools had gained a reputation for being experimental and adopted some radical approaches to education. One young girl named Anne, returning from Canada with her sister Suzette, was astounded when she visited one such outlandish school with her mother:

> We were advised that Dartington Hall had a reputation as an experimental, progressive form of education, and without questioning that description further my parents thought that after the rather free way of life in Canada it might suit Suzette rather well. In any event in August we set off for Devon by train having made an appointment for a certain morning with the headmaster Mr W.B. Curry. We were not aware of the specific nature of the school or what kind of experiments it professed. If we had known

we probably wouldn't have gone. Mr Curry conducted the interview by outlining the purpose and functions of the school according to his philosophy of freedom and self-government; co-education, or co-habitation might have been a more accurate word, involving full participation by the students in every facet of life. At this time little importance was given to preparing them for the school certificate. Scholastics and academics were secondary to the arts, and free expression and individual development of each child.

After this introductory talk Mr Curry offered to show us around the school buildings and groups. It was a beautiful place in a lovely setting. The open air swimming pool was on the tour of course, and here the significance of what we had been hearing about the school's philosophy was borne out in no unmistakable terms. At one end of the pool were the changing rooms and it struck us immediately that there was no separate accommodation for boys and girls. My mother queried the reason for, what seemed to her, these very inadequate arrangements, and it was then that Mr Curry explained that it was customary for the children to swim in the nude, that it was policy not to have segregation of the sexes in any way, and therefore it was totally unnecessary to have separate changing rooms.

My mother ventured to voice her concern that she didn't think her fourteen-year-old daughter would like swimming about without her bathing costume on. Mr Curry assured her that it would be quite permissible for her to wear it, but soon, he felt sure, she would begin to feel strange as the odd one out, and freely divest herself of it. After this startling revelation we bade our goodbyes and on reporting all this to my father, with a certain amount of merriment I might add, it was decided that Dartington Hall, or perhaps any co-ed boarding school, was not the answer.[13]

Choosing between a rigid state education system and a radical private system was clearly not an option for some returnees, and wealthy parents tended to send their offspring to traditional private schools with proven academic track records.

Dominion accents, culture, sport, food, schooling and levels of health all continued to set the newly returned children apart from their native counterparts. They were taller and heavier, with healthy rosy cheeks and suntanned skin. In addition to the overall resentment, they experienced difficulties in schools because of curriculum differences, and they found British houses dingy, small, old-fashioned and poorly-built compared to the large, open-plan houses in the Dominions. They missed the sunshine and the open-air lifestyles. Britain appeared grey and dismal by comparison. As a consequence, some children simply failed to settle, as the mother of Heather Johnston noted:

Heather was only eleven years old when she returned and didn't know me. She cried every time she got a letter from New Zealand, and, as I still had to go out to work, there was no warm welcome for her when she came home from school. Also food and fuel were hard to come by, which was not in my favour. She longed to return to New Zealand. When she was fifteen, a new scheme was started by the U.K. government to enable any evacuees to return, so I reluctantly let her go. She returned to her foster parents and was very happy – and so were they. I came out to New Zealand after my mother died in 1959. I have since returned for visits to the UK. My heart is there; but my home is in New Zealand now.[14]

The foster mother of a young girl named Joan also recalled that her evacuee failed to settle back in England:

After the war had ended, Joan became very unsettled and unhappy about the prospect of returning to her parents, and her headmistress said that she was equally unsettled at school. Joan had only been seven years old when she was evacuated. She had forgotten her parents and was very upset when she left us. She was still only twelve years old, and we feel it was a very traumatic experience for her. During her time with us, we had a son and a daughter, and she regarded us all as her own family..........Joan failed to settle in England and her mother said 'Life was so different for her and she couldn't adjust. We had a difficult time with her for three or four years. In fact, it continued until she was married just before seventeen years old. Twenty-three years later, still cherishing her evacuation days, Joan returned to settle in her host country with her husband and children.[15]

Mr Philip Robinson also shared this longing to leave England and return to his host country:

I tried for years to persuade my wife to emigrate to Australia, but she was an English girl with very deep roots. But in 1977 I had the opportunity to go to Australia for a holiday. I came over on my own, and met the family again – the welcome I got you just wouldn't believe! I came over again in 1984. My wife was ill and I had been advised to disappear for a few weeks, but she died a few months after I returned. My mother was still living in England. She was nearly ninety and I felt I had to stay there and look after her. Ironically all her relatives lived in Australia. She died in 1987. I was suddenly relieved of all my obligations. The dilemma arose, should I come to live in Australia or shouldn't I? I couldn't make up my mind so I went to the local village church to plead for guidance. The feeling came over me that if I could find anything in that church which was connected to Australia then I should come. I was drawn to the visitor's book. The last person to have signed that visitor's book came from Melbourne, from the suburb next to where my cousin lives. So I bought a ticket and came.[16]

Undoubtedly there were many sea-vacs who harboured dreams of returning to their host countries and were unable to do so because of family commitments, and experienced resettlement problems as a result. Moreover, there was no government support or guidance for children returning from overseas. However, there is evidence that local social service departments provided at least an initial service in terms of meeting children from ports and escorting them to their various destinations. The following letter was written to Bristol social services department by Mr G.L. Boyle in 1944:

Dear Sir

I cannot say how grateful my wife and I are for the great service you rendered us when the children arrived back in England. It was quite an experience for them both and had it not been for your kind offices when they landed at Bristol I feel sure they would have suffered considerable distress of mind. I would also like to thank the gentleman who, at a moments notice, accompanied the children to Paddington. It was an example of real Christianity in practice.[17]

Not all return journeys were predictable and some children had no idea when or how they would reach England, or indeed where they would arrive. Parents were often required to contact several points of arrival in the hope of obtaining assistance for their onward journeys. The Director of Bristol Social Services received the following vague letter:

Dear Sir

Anthony and David Carr

Information has been received that the above-mentioned boys who were privately evacuated are expected to arrive in this country from the USA in the near future, probably on a naval craft. No information is available as to the port at which the boys may arrive, but if they should arrive at your port I shall be glad if you will arrange for them to be met and if necessary provided with accommodation temporarily. The parents are anxious to meet the boys at any London station indicated, but do not want them to

be sent to Windsor by any other route. Any expenses incurred on the boys'
behalf should be claimed by the parents and no doubt you will inform this
office on the event of their arrival.[18]

Those returning from overseas frequently found it difficult to readjust to home
life and expressed feelings of dislocation and isolation; public sympathy was
in short supply. Official CORB reports claimed that schools and welfare systems were sympathetic towards the needs of these children but this was not
the case. A few politicians suggested that a health-related survey of returning
sea-vacs could prove to be interesting, but there was no widespread support
for such action and the suggestion was quashed. Yet the British government
was eager to help those children and their families who wished to stay in the
Dominions, or to emigrate from Britain after the war. Indeed, the idea of helping British parents of sea-vacs to relocate overseas was first proposed in 1942
in an internal CORB Memo.[19] The benefits of keeping children and possibly
their families overseas were obvious. During the initial post-war years rationing was still in place and returning evacuees would put an extra strain on
food supplies. Furthermore, there were acute housing shortages with thousands of people living in makeshift tents because of the Blitz. Representatives
from the Ministry of Labour also pointed out that emigration schemes would
ease the demobilisation process and reduce the risk of post-war unemploy-
ment. Emigrants were therefore offered free passages and financial assistance
to set up homes in the Dominions.[20]

Applications from CORB evacuees and their families to settle overseas
were given priority by the receiving nations. These emigrants were also
helped by family and host family connections, and in many cases host parents who were bereft at the loss of their evacuee children set about finding
homes and employment for their biological parents. Upon their arrival in the
Dominions sea-vacs and their families were simply absorbed into existing
family networks. By December 1946 over 30 per cent of sea-vacs had emigrated to the Dominions. This percentage rose steadily until the late 1960s.

Notes

1   National Archive D.O.131/27 Final Report of the CORB Advisory Council 22
    February 1946.
2   The private papers of J.B. Wells, held at the Imperial War Museum ref: 67/233/1.
3   Fethney, M., *The Absurd and the Brave* (1990) p.233.
4   Memoirs of Roy Unwins, documented for the BBC. www.bbc.ww2peopleswar.
5   Parsons, M. & Starns, P., *The Evacuation: The True Story* (1999) p. 176.
6   *Ibid.* p. 177.

7 Stokes, E., *Innocents Abroad* (1994) p.199.

8 *Ibid.* p. 196.

9 *Ibid.*

10 Fethney, M., *The Absurd and the Brave* (1990) p. 237.

11 Schiff. J.A., 'Yale's Foster Children' *Yale Alumni* July 2010.

12 Lin, P., 'National Identity and Social Mobility: Class, Empire and the British Government Overseas Evacuation of Children During the Second World War', *Twentieth Century British History* vol. 7, no. 3 (1996) pp. 335–6.

13 Private papers of Mrs Anne Winter (née Westcott) evacuated to Canada accompanied by her mother and sister via Furness Withey shipping company in 1940, returned 1944. Imperial War Museum ref. 91/37/1.

14 Fethney, M. *Absurd and the Brave* (1990) p. 250.

15 *Ibid.* p. 249.

16 Stokes, E., *Innocents Abroad* (1994) p. 210.

17 Bristol County Record Office, letter to Bristol Social Services Department from G.L. Boyle of Cavendish Rd Cambridge, 19 November 1944.

18 Bristol County Record Office, letter to the Director of Social Services from the Ministry of Health Regional Office Bristol 8, 28 November 1944.

19 National Archive DO131/35 CORB Internal Memo 13 August 1942.

20 *Ibid.*

14

Success or Failure

The success or failure of children's overseas evacuation schemes can be gauged to a large extent by assessing the political objectives and parental expectations that were associated with the programmes. They can also be measured by looking at the short- and long-term impact they had on the children concerned, the number of times such children were relocated and the length of time they spent in each home. Certainly in terms of relocation rates the overseas schemes appear to have been more successful than the internal domestic evacuation, but this was not necessarily the case. While it was true that there was not quite the same degree of class conflict in the Dominions and America, and greater stress was placed on a sense of 'Britishness', as children from the 'mother country,' overseas evacuees nonetheless experienced the same emotional trauma as those who had remained on the home front. The overseas scheme merely appeared to be more successful in this sense because 63 per cent of all CORB children actually went to live with relatives or friends recommended by their parents. The relocation of the remainder echoed domestic evacuation in that 30 per cent were removed from their original host families and only 7 per cent of these were successfully placed for the duration of the war. In reality children evacuated overseas were far more likely to stay put with their host families simply because it was far too difficult, expensive and time-consuming for the biological parents to travel abroad and retrieve their offspring. Most had sent their children abroad for safekeeping and in the hope that they would receive better educational opportunities in foreign lands; to this extent most had achieved their objectives. Politicians, meanwhile, had nurtured other objectives. At best they had viewed CORB children as ambassadors for Britain and potential saviours, and at worst they had dismissed them out of hand as useless mouths.[1]

It is reasonable to suggest that as ambassadors for Britain the children did their utmost to adopt the role and behave appropriately, especially in public. They often regarded media attention as a nuisance but endured it without complaint. The older children were more aware of their propaganda roles, but younger children also displayed an astute level of political understanding beyond their years. They were aware that a stoical and brave façade was needed to highlight Britain's war needs and they usually managed to look cheerful in all the endless photographs that were taken by photo-journalists. Even children who were unhappy with their host families usually bore their suffering silently and put on a brave face. British politicians hoped that children would tug at the public heartstrings and to a large extent they did. Newspaper articles entitled 'Little Bundles from War Torn Britain,' 'British Children Give the Thumbs up,' 'Children from the Mother Country,' and 'Britain's Precious Heritage' continually gave the sea-vacs a high public profile. Comic strip stories entitled the 'Adventures of Sea-vacs,' and 'Sea-vacs Spot the Enemy' also served to focus attention on the plight of British children who were travelling the expanse of oceans in order to find a safe haven. Reporting on the arrival of 5,000 British children in America, newspapers pointed out that these children had seen people dying and injured and had experienced anxiety, terror, grief, hunger and fatigue.[2] Nevertheless, public sympathy for sea-vacs did not equate with political action. For example, members of the British War Cabinet had hoped that the arrival of British children in America in 1940 would sway public and political opinion, and persuade America to enter the war by joining forces with Britain. The overriding belief in American Congress, however, was that Britain was trying to provoke an international incident in order to force America into the war. However, the British government had insisted on safe passage guarantees both on outward and homecoming journeys. Therefore, although some scholars have erroneously suggested that a few British politicians were willing to gamble children's lives on the possibility of getting America into the war, this was not the case.[3] Moreover, in the face of this belief, however unfounded, Congressmen were more likely to dig their heels in than alter attitudes towards war in Europe. Thus although the presence of CORB children and other British children was a constant reminder of Britain's dilemma, it is doubtful that this presence had any real impact on the foreign policies of the countries concerned. As ambassadors for Britain, therefore, the role of CORB children was severely limited.

The sea-vacs' role as useless mouths also resonated with politicians at home and abroad. It is estimated that over 30,000 women and children took refuge overseas for the duration of the war, most of them without CORB assistance. Undoubtedly this number, had they remained at home, would have placed extra pressure on Britain's already limited resources. However, it was wholly inaccurate for politicians to describe these women and children as useless mouths since they would have formed an integral part of the war effort, working on farms and in factories.

To assume that CORB children would become potential saviours in the event of a German invasion of Britain was also a rather far-fetched notion. Fortunately for Britain they were not called upon to fulfil this role. None of the children interviewed in the Lin study or in subsequent research studies had ever contemplated the fact that they might have been required to fight to regain fortress Britain. Indeed, at the end of the war a third of returning evacuees from Canada met with CORB representatives with a view to resettling in Canada, and another third wished to do so if escorted by relatives.[4] Given the eagerness with which CORB children rushed to resettle abroad, it was highly unlikely that they would have taken up the British cause in the event of a German takeover, although Dominion armed forces would have undoubtedly fought for the recovery of Britain had it been necessary to do so; in fact, Prime Minister Winston Churchill asserted as much in his rallying and inspiring speeches. For individual sea-vacs however, nothing was further from their minds. The famous British philosopher and SS *City of Benares* survivor Lord Quinton is just one of the evacuees who believed that had *City of Benares* made it to Canada, he would not have returned to his homeland:

> I should probably have gone into the insurance business, other people seem to go in of my type in Canada and I would be a very vigorous member of Friendly Societies and Rotary and things of that sort. I think I would have turned in to an entirely different sort of person.[5]

Those who did manage to reach their destinations very often launched themselves into new lifestyles with enthusiasm. There was no room in their thoughts for the prospect of having to fight another day for their homeland. As potential saviours therefore, sea-vacs were nonentities.

The failure of political objectives however, did not detract from the fact that the overseas evacuation scheme had provided thousands of children with new opportunities and a new perspective on life. But for many the trauma and social dislocation of returning was probably worse than their departure. They were simply expected to adapt and get on with everyday living, as though the previous six years had been a mere hiatus in their upbringing. Moreover the stark contrast between living standards in Britain and those in America and the Dominions were emphasised in their personal recollections:

When I arrived back from Canada there was nothing left of our street, the whole family had to go and live at my Aunt's house because at least it was still standing even if it looked like it should be condemned. Everything about England even the people seemed drab and shabby compared with what I'd been used to. I felt as though I didn't belong anymore. Six years is a long time out of a child's life. I never properly fitted in with the family again.[6]

We'd had plenty of food in Australia and lots of open spaces to play. People seemed more relaxed and friendly. When I got back home everyone seemed weary and there was no nice food, you know – treats or anything. I began to feel very guilty because my family had had such a bad time and I had been quite unaware really. I didn't want to tell them how happy I'd been when I was away so I didn't tell them anything at all. They just thought I'd become a moody teenager.[7]

Dysfunctional family networks were a legacy of evacuation generally, and in terms of emotional problems the percentage of children requiring professional child guidance after the war was roughly the same for both internal, domestic evacuees and their overseas counterparts. Parents had agreed to the evacuation of their children as a means to keep them safe, but children often interpreted this action as an act of abandonment. The real departure of the ways when examining the legacy of overseas evacuation can be found in the social mobility of children. All research studies have revealed that children who were evacuated overseas fared better socially and economically, both at home and abroad. Certainly a large proportion of sea-vacs returned to their host country and did very well in their chosen careers but as Lin's study concluded:

In the long run emigration was not a prerequisite for social and occupational advancement. Although many evacuees who emigrated were socially mobile, such as Jean Arkwright, the daughter of a York machinist who was hosted by an accountant's family in Ontario, Canada and became a lab technician after resettling in Canada, Timothy Weston, the son of a Newcastle upon Tyne bus conductor who was hosted by a Canadian farmer and became a pharmacist, and George Broder, the son of a Norwich horse stableman who was hosted by a corporate treasurer in Ontario, Canada and became a chemical engineer at the management level after also returning to his host country, so were many who chose to remain in Britain. For example, the cases of Thomas Fielding the son of a Bradford clerk who was hosted by a doctor's family in Australia, and became a headmaster, Doreen Glance, the daughter of a steel mill worker who was hosted by a wholesale butcher also in Australia, and became a tax officer, and Jean Myles, the daughter of a London mill worker who was evacuated to Canada and became a nurse. Indeed, in my sample, both non-emigrant CORB evacuees and CORB evacuees as a whole attained much higher levels of educational and social/occupational achievement than their peers who were not evacuated overseas.[8]

In addition to the upwardly mobile effects of overseas evacuation there was also a rise in the uptake of Dominion-sponsored emigration schemes in the 1950s and '60s. Whereas before the war travel abroad was virtually unheard of, particularly within the working classes, there was widespread public support for emigration schemes after the war. Faced with a war-damaged Britain and continued austerity measures, it was no wonder that emigration became an attractive option for many. As children chattered endlessly about their host nations and exaggerated their benefits – claiming that the sun always shone in America and the Dominions, food was always plentiful and the people always welcoming – their parents and often their extended families began to consider the prospect of settling overseas. Foreign lands were no longer an unknown quantity to be viewed with suspicion but places that had welcomed British children with open arms during a time of crisis. The lack of rigid class boundaries overseas also played a part in the decision-making process. In the Dominions and in America people were more likely to be viewed in terms of their skills and aptitude rather than by their social class. These were nations that arguably allowed meritocracy to rule the day in terms of employment opportunities.[9] It should be noted, however, that these opportunities were not normally available to races that were not of pure European descent. Governments in receiving countries operated either a covert or an overt colour bar.

The popularity of emigration schemes was also a concern for the British government. On the one hand government ministers were happy for British children's charities to send thousands of orphans to the Dominions, but on the other hand they were not so happy to support adult and family emigration schemes.[10] The birth rate had declined sharply during the war, and post-war Britain was suffering from acute labour shortages. When the issue of emigration was debated in the House of Commons there were no clear outcomes and no set policy directives for some time. CORB officials had long since recognised that a large proportion of their children would want to settle in their host countries, and to this end they had offered them advice and financial assistance. They had sold the idea to parliament on the basis that it would prevent a recurrence of the massive employment problems that were experienced by rapid demobilisation at the end of the First World War. Circumstances were very different at the end of the Second World War, however, partly because of the bomb damage that had occurred on the home front and partly because post-war British commitments in the Middle East prevented a rapid demobilisation of troops. But young people were needed to rebuild Britain after the war and several MPs, such as the social reformer Miss Eleanor Rathbone, were worried that emigration schemes would considerably worsen the situation by encouraging youthful men and their families to desert Britain.[11] The Prime Minister endorsed this view. In response to British concerns, therefore, the Dominion governments eventually extended the age limit for emigration to 45 years. Subsequently a rather strange scenario developed whereby the British government actively encouraged immigration from all populations of the Empire while simultaneously providing financial assistance to emigration schemes. This two-way population flow gives some credence to Geoffrey Shakespeare's initial hope that Britain and her Empire would be more closely intertwined socially and economically as a result of overseas evacuation.

For those sea-vacs and their families who rejected emigration in favour of picking up the threads of their lives in Britain, over 70 per cent kept in touch with their host families, usually by regular correspondence and intermittent telephone conversations. A long-term legacy of overseas evacuation therefore, was the forging of lifelong friendships. Marjorie Ursell, for example, remained in communication with her host parents in Australia for over forty years: 'The mother wrote to me for years on my return, and then the father when she died. The rest of the family never kept in touch and though I know they all married, and some even visited here but I have not seen them since.'[12]

For those who were more affluent, friendships links were maintained by reciprocal visits. Academic American families, for instance, were invited by British academics to visit Oxford and Cambridge via schemes. Anna Miles Jones was a sibling in a host family and recalled that:

The fourteen-year-old daughter of Oxford zoology Professor John Baker came to Yale with the Oxford evacuees and lived in our household for several years. My father was Walter Miles, Professor of physiological psychology, and my mother Catherine Cox Miles, was Clinical Professor of psychology, both at Yale School of Medicine. Venice [daughter of John Baker] and her family and I and my family have remained quite close in the intervening years. In gratitude, Oxford arranged for the children of Yale host families to spend a summer in Oxford in 1950. My husband joined me (using the G.I. Bill) for that wonderful summer studying, pub crawling, and sightseeing; a glorious memory.[13]

Appreciative and generous British parents often clubbed together and organised fundraising events in order to accrue enough money to host American and Dominion families. Relationships across the oceans also did much to encourage tolerance of individual cultures and in many quarters raised social and economic expectations. Indeed, the impact of overseas evacuation reverberated down through generations. Lynn Codd, the daughter of a Tyneside ship polisher, returned to England aged 16 hoping to take advantage of the education she had received in Canada. Tutors had recommended that she should attend university, but her father protested against such a pathway and she remained working class. Nevertheless, she passed on the educational values she had gained in Canada to her son:

> I raised my son, an only child, to appreciate the good things in life, to take advantage of a good education with all the benefits it could bring, to enjoy learning, to be an achiever and to be self reliant. He went on to get a law degree and then to become a barrister, which is a profession normally associated for the middle and upper classes.[14]

From an intellectual, social and occupational standpoint there is no doubt that sea-vacs fared extremely well and far better than children who had remained in Britain. Emotionally however, the trauma of being separated from parents impacted in much the same way in both groups. As adults a large number of these were able to enter occupations like psychology and use their experiences to help others who were traumatised. But some traumatised children could never come to terms with their evacuation years and carried their trauma into adulthood. Others managed to suppress their emotions. Lord Quinton, for example, believed that he was totally unscathed by the disastrous sinking of the SS *City of Benares*, until his nightmares told him otherwise:

> At school I thought it hadn't had any real effect on me, I mean I didn't think about its effect and I slept well and ate vehemently and all the rest of it but my pals in my dormitory said I used to make an awful lot of noise at night. I went in for shouting and that, so I probably sustained a good deal of unconscious distress from the whole thing but it didn't leave any lasting marks as far as I know.[15]

Frank Brookshaw of the HMS *Anthony* also suffered from sleep disorders: 'I've had many sleepless nights. A man can look after himself, but when it's a woman or a child what hope of they got in situations like that? They were little heroes. It taught me a lot in life.'[16]

Overseas evacuation was undoubtedly riddled with tragedies and traumas that left substantial emotional scars on the families concerned, particularly in the short term. Yet in the long term, and the final analysis, the overseas evacuation of children was extraordinarily successful. In addition to socio-economic advantages, the evacuation schemes had brought children into the public limelight and prompted international social reform within each receiving country. The Canadian government even thanked the British government formally after the war, because the sending of British children had encouraged the development of coherent child welfare programmes across the provinces for the first time in Canadian history. The remaining Dominions and America also stepped up to the mark and introduced wide-spread social reform in the field of child welfare.

On the home front, the dismal failure of evacuation had prompted national reform in the shape of the Butler Education Act of 1944, The Children's Act of 1948 and the emergence of the Welfare State. Overseas evacuation schemes, meanwhile, were instrumental in establishing international guidelines for child welfare. Rules were introduced to safeguard children worldwide through the United Nations Declaration of Human Rights, the International Red Cross and a wide variety of international children's charities and organisations. There was a greater emphasis on child psychology and pioneers in this field drew on the experiences of all children caught up in conflict situations. The post-war introduction of child welfare clinics across the world was arguably the result of all child evacuation schemes.

Children involved in domestic evacuation schemes had been beaten down with the circumstances of war, the prolonged bombing campaigns and the deadly pilotless V1 and V2 rockets. Most of them had viewed the war from the ringside seats of the cities and been subject to the stringent rules of food rationing, the inconvenience of black out conditions, and a lack of adequate education.[17] The sea-vacs, in sharp contrast had returned to Britain well educated, somewhat shocked by conditions on the home front, but with the easy confidence of seasoned travellers. They were unfairly told by many that they were cowards who had run away from war. Identified by their Dominion accents they were outwardly harassed, targeted for discrimination and hindered in their attempts to fulfil the career goals they had established while abroad.[18] It was not, therefore, surprising that many of them simply wished to return to their host countries as soon as possible. In comparison to domestic evacuees, the majority of sea-vacs were affectionately drawn into homes in the Dominions and America. They were cosseted and overwhelmed with presents and generosity, pampered, feted, and generally well cared for.

However, sea-vacs maintained that the overriding legacy of overseas evacuation for them was the sense of tolerance, freedom and independence they had developed whilst living in other countries. Their experiences gave them a broader outlook on life and wider horizons in terms of what could be achieved in life. These attitudes were passed on from generation to generation and therefore had a significant long term social impact. For healthcare professionals, young sea-vacs and domestic evacuees provided new information in terms of charting a child's psychological development. As Anna Freud pointed out: 'We were trying so hard to be of psychological assistance to those children, but I have to say, they were of great assistance to us. We learned about the stresses placed on the young by war, but we also learned about the agility and resourcefulness of children.'[19]

Perhaps the most surprising aspect of overseas evacuation was the myriad ways in which child evacuees successfully negotiated their relationships both with host and biological parents in a remarkably adult manner. They would often keep their own counsel when they deemed it necessary, and would frequently put the needs of others before their own. For the most part they behaved exceptionally well and made the best of the opportunities afforded them. Even those who suffered psychologically from homesickness, neglect or abuse still achieved more educationally and occupationally than the children who were left on the home front. From a psychological standpoint it has been observed that a healthy adult brings life experience, cultural beliefs, established support relationships and emotional resources to the task. A child is in the midst of developing those resources; navigating the world depends upon the love, support, and education provided by parents and caregivers.[20] The standard of parenting skills varied tremendously in America and across the Dominions, and some children were undoubtedly more resilient than others, but it can be argued that since most children evacuated overseas experienced the immense trauma of separation from their biological parents, and then six years later from their host parents, they were more likely to suffer from separation anxiety as they got older than their domestic counterparts.

Indeed, if success or failure is measured in terms of the level of psychological trauma caused by parent–child separations, then overseas evacuation schemes were on a par with domestic evacuation schemes, since both programmes failed to predict or acknowledge the degree to which the evacuation process generated emotional distress in children. However, if success is measured by the degree of educational attainment, social mobility and economic achievements that were gained by British children both during and after the war, then the overseas evacuation schemes were enormously successful. Finally, it is worth remembering that, in the midst of the much publicised exploitative and forced child migration schemes that took place either side of the Second World War, during the war thousands of British children were given wonderful, loving and caring homes in America and the Dominions at a time of utmost need.

Notes

1 Starns, P., *The Evacuation of Children During World War Two* (2004) pp. 59–60.
2 The History of the USA's Children's Bureau *www.socialwelfarehistory.com/organizations.com*
3 Jackson, C., *Who Will Take Our Children?* (1985) chapters 3–6.
4 Lin, P., 'National Identity and Social Mobility; Class, Empire and the British Government Overseas Evacuation of Children During the Second World War.' *Twentieth Century British History*, vol.7 No. 3 (1996) p 337.
5 Lord Quinton interviewed for the BBC 1999, quoted in Parsons, M. & Starns, P., *The Evacuation: The True Story* (1999) p. 163.
6 Starns, P. *The Evacuation of Children During World War Two* (2004) p. 122.
7 *Ibid.*
8 Lin, P., 'National Identity and Social Mobility, Class, Empire and the British Government Overseas Evacuation of Children During World War Two' *Twentieth Century British History* vol. 7, No. 3, (1996) p. 337.
9 Meritocracy as a prerequisite for employment did not really emerge in Britain until the late 1960s and early 1970s. It was in part signalled by the formation of the Open University, which opened its doors to students in 1971.
10 Wagner, G., *Children of the Empire* (1982).
11 Hansard House of Commons Parliamentary Debates 5th Series, Miss Rathbone speaking to the House of Commons, 22 February 1945.
12 Private papers of Marjorie Ursell held at the Imperial War Museum ref: 96/55/1.
13 Miles Jones, A., Letter to Yale Alumni, July 2010.
14 Lin, P., P. Lin Collection, Imperial War Museum, questionnaire 64.
15 Lord Quinton, oral history interview for the BBC in 1999 quoted in Parsons, M. & Starns, P., *The Evacuation: The True Story* (1999) p. 152.
16 Frank Brookshaw interviewed for the BBC in 1999, quoted in Parsons, M. & Starns, P., *The Evacuation: The True Story* (1999) p. 167.
17 Starns, P., *Blitz Families: The Children Who Stayed Behind* (2012).
18 Lin, P. 'National Identity and Social Mobility, Class, Empire and the British Government Overseas Evacuation of Children During World War Two' in *Twentieth Century British History* Vol. 7 No. 3 (1996) p. 335.
19 Freud, A. & Burlingham, D., *War and Children* (1943)
20 Erikson, C.B. & Rupp, E. A., 'Bereavement in a War Zone' in Marten, J. (ed.) *Children and War* (2002) p. 87.

Bibliography

Barker, R., *Children of the Benares* (1987)

Bilson, G., *Guest Children* (1988)

Calder, A., *The People's War* (1971)

Erikson, C.B. & Rupp, E.A., 'Bereavement in a War Zone' in Marten, J. (ed), *Children and War* (2002)

Fethney, M., *The Absurd and the Brave* (1990)

Freud, A. & Burlingham, D., *War and Children* (1943)

Huxley, E., *Atlantic Ordeal: The Story of Mary Cornish* (1941)

Inglis, R., *The Children's War* (1989)

Jackson, C., *Who Will Take Our Children?* (1985)

Johnson, D.E., *Exodus of Children* (1985)

Mann, J., *Out of Harm's Way* (2005)

Menzies, J., *Children of the Doomed Voyage* (2005)

Parsons, M. & Starns, P., *The Evacuation – The True Story* (1999)

Shakespeare, G., *Let Candles Be Brought In* (1949)

Starns, P., *Blitz Families: The Children Who Stayed Behind* (2012)

Stokes, E., *Innocents Abroad* (1994)

Wagner, G., *Children of the Empire* (1982)

Index

American Committee for the Evacuation of European Children 40, 41, 55, 62, 89, 92
American Red Cross 60
Anselm 35
Anthony 50
*Arandora Star , SS*30
Attlee, C. 100

Batory 36, 37
Battle of Britain 64, 66
Bayano 80
Beamish, Rear Admiral 14
Biddle, E. 58
Blair, E.C. 98
Braithwaite, Major 15
British Eugenics Society 39, 40
British Expeditionary Force 17
Brittain, V. 66
Brookshaw, F. 52, 152
Butler Education Act 140, 153

Canadian Council for Overseas Children 101
Canadian Eugenics Society 39, 40
Canadian Income Tax Act 101

Canadian National Council of Education 98
Canadian National Registration of Women for War Work 41
Canadian Welfare Council 100
Canadian Women's War Service Committee 101
Carmine 92
Caruccia 92
Chamberlain, N. 17
Child and Parent Settlement Scheme 117
Children's Act 1948 153
Children's Overseas Reception Board (CORB) 10, 11, 20, 21, 22, 24, 25, 26, 27, 28, 29, 30, 31, 34, 36, 38, 39, 40, 41, 43, 46, 50, 54, 55, 56, 75, 77, 82, 84, 88, 98, 100, 101, 102, 103, 105, 106, 107, 108, 110, 111, 113, 114, 115, 116, 117, 118, 119, 120, 123, 124, 126, 132, 134, 135, 137, 144, 146, 147, 148, 150
Churchill, W., Prime Minister 17, 18, 19, 22, 23, 54, 60, 64, 148

City of Benares 46, 47, 49, 50, 53, 54, 55, 62, 73, 148, 152
Collins, J. 53
concentration camps 31
Cunningham, G. 43

Dominions Office Supply Committee 14
Duchess of Atholl 70
Duchess of York 104
Dunkirk 17
Dutch profiteering 29, 34

Einstein, A. 65

Foll, H.S. Senator 109, 112
Ford Motor Company 10, 15, 41, 60
Freud, A. 154

Garnett, W.J. 108, 119
Gilbert, M. Sir 76

Hankey, M. 22
Haw Haw, Lord 22
Hitler, A. 33, 40, 46, 59
Hoover, H. 60, 62
Hoover Vacuum Company 15
Hurricane 47, 50, 53
Hutton, Dr 40

International Red Cross 152

Jeffs, H.B. 99
Johnson, J. 71, 72, 73, 75

King, M. 98
Kodak Photographic Company 10, 15, 41, 60

Llanstephan Castle 73, 74
Lothian, Lord 29

Luftwaffe 36
Lunn, M.P. for Rothwell 34, 35

Mackinnon, Admiral 54
Maxse, M. 21, 100, 105, 106, 123, 137
medical defects 34, 35
medical screening 27, 28, 34, 35, 40, 62, 74, 99, 101, 102, 104
Mercy Ship Bill 28
Mercy Ship Scheme 28, 29, 58, 60
Ministry of Transport 30
Ministry of War 30
Mullins, A. 21

National Child Refugee Committee 59
Nerissa 87
Nestor 75
New Zealand Children's Emergency Regulations 118
New Zealand National Department of Education 118
Ney, E.J., Major 98

O'Sullivan, R. 51

Priestly, J.B. 15

Quinton, Lord 48, 49, 148, 152

Rangitata 118, 119
Roosevelt, E. 59, 60, 61
Roosevelt, F.D. President 28
Ruanhine 71, 72, 73, 118, 135
Ryder-Richardson, C. 52

Samaria 63, 92,
Scythia 63, 92
Shakespeare, G. 11, 17, 19, 20, 21, 22, 24, 25, 26, 28, 29, 30, 33,

34, 36, 37, 38, 41, 42, 43, 44,
50, 53, 54, 56, 61, 62, 77, 80,
81, 82, 89, 90, 93, 123, 151
Shaw, E. Captain 50
Social Darwinism 40
South African Control and Care of
Overseas Children 126
South African National Advisory
Committee of Overseas Children's
Administration 126

Temporary Migration of Children
Act 99

United Nations Declaration of
Human Rights 153
United States of America Committee
for the Care of European Children
59

Vancouver deaf and blind school
102
Victory in Europe celebrations 116
Volandem 36, 37, 44, 46

War Cabinet 17, 30, 56, 147
Warner Brothers 15
Wear, M. 39, 40
Wedgewood-Benn, D. 18
Wellington City Young Britons
Committee 119
Western Prince 63
Whitton, C. 100
Williams, S., Baroness 66
Wilshaw, E., Sir 82
Winchelsea 47

Youth Settlement Scheme 123

Lightning Source UK Ltd.
Milton Keynes UK
UKOW03f2359100114

224367UK00002B/5/P

9 780752 490113